Cambridge Latin Course

Units IIA and

Teacher's Handbook

Second edition

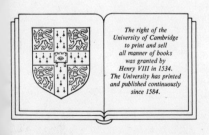

The right of the University of Cambridge to print and sell all manner of books was granted by Henry VIII in 1534. The University has printed and published continuously since 1584.

CAMBRIDGE UNIVERSITY PRESS

Cambridge

London   New York   New Rochelle

Melbourne   Sydney

Published by the Press Syndicate of the University of Cambridge
The Pitt Building, Trumpington Street, Cambridge CB2 1RP
32 East 57th Street, New York, NY 10022, USA
10 Stamford Road, Oakleigh, Melbourne 3166, Australia

This book, an outcome of work jointly commissioned by the Schools Council
before its closure and the Cambridge School Classics Project, is published
under the aegis of the School Curriculum Development Committee,
Newcombe House, 45 Notting Hill Gate, London W11 3JB.

First published 1971
Second edition 1983
Reprinted 1985

Printed in Great Britain at the University Press, Cambridge

ISBN 0 521 28745 6

Contents

Preface

For help in the preparation of Units IIA and IIB in their revised form, we should like to record our continued indebtedness to members of the Project team, editorial staff of the Cambridge University Press, the Project's Advisory Panel and others who were named and thanked in the Preface to the Unit I Handbook. In addition, we should like to thank, for assistance of various kinds, Roger Davies, Mark Greenstock, Nick Lowe, Chris McLeod, Betty Munday, Nick Munday and Sally Reeve.

D.J. Morton	Director
E.P. Story	Deputy Director
R.M. Griffin	Revision Editor
Cambridge School Classics Project	

Cambridge 1983

Unit IIA

Introduction

Unit IIA (Stages 13–16) of the Cambridge Latin Course was designed in accordance with the aims and principles described in the Unit I Teacher's Handbook (pp.2–4). For general advice on teaching method, teachers are referred to Unit I Handbook pp.15–27; detailed suggestions are given in the stage commentaries which follow this introduction.

As before, the reading material makes use wherever possible of historical characters and situations illustrative of Roman life in the first century A.D. Unit IIA is set in Roman Britain, three years after the events of Unit I. Some continuity with Unit I is provided through Quintus, the son of Caecilius Iucundus. The chief characters of Unit IIA are portrayed in rather fuller detail than the simple stereotypes of Unit I, and the stage commentaries include occasional suggestions for discussion of these characters and their behaviour, as well as for exploration of the various aspects of Romano-British life reflected in the material.

A Language Information pamphlet is published with Unit IIA. Like the corresponding pamphlet for Unit I, it contains a reference vocabulary for the whole Unit, and an 'About the language' section intended both for reference and for consolidation work.

In Unit IIA, such items as the infinitive, relative clauses and the pluperfect tense are introduced into the reading material. But the linguistic emphasis falls less on the introduction of new features than on the consolidation and practice of features already met in Unit I, including some (such as the adjective) which appeared in the Unit I reading material without being commented on. The morphology of the noun and verb is practised in the stage exercises and in the Language Information pamphlet. The stage exercises tend to focus particularly on the noun; the Language Information exercises put slightly more emphasis on the verb. The suggestions for oral work in the stage commentaries below are concerned especially with the verb and the adjective.

It was suggested in the Unit I Handbook (p.9) that in a four-year course Units I, IIA and IIB should normally constitute the first year's work. Some or all of the following passages in Unit IIA might be read quickly or omitted by those whose time allowance is short:

Stage 13   'Salvius fundum īnspicit'
Stage 14   'Rūfilla cubiculum ōrnat' and 'Quīntus advenit'
Stage 15   'lūdī fūnebrēs'

If a passage is omitted altogether, it is usually advisable to give the pupils a brief résumé of its content.

Filmstrip and cassette

Cambridge Classical Filmstrip 2, 'Roman Britain', contains visual material suitable for use with Units IIA and IIIA. It includes the following topics (asterisks indicate frames of particular relevance to Unit IIA):

*Title frame–1	The conquest
* 2–14	Romanisation
*15–22	Daily life
23–29	Religion
30–35	The army

In this Handbook, reference to particular frames is given by filmstrip frame number, and also (where appropriate) by slide number for the benefit of those teachers who are using the slides which accompanied the first edition of the course. Unless otherwise stated, references are to Filmstrip 2 and Unit II slides.

The first cassette accompanying the course includes the following material from Unit IIA:

Stage 13	'trēs servī'
Stage 14	'Domitilla cubiculum parat'
	'in tablīnō'
Stage 15	'lūdī fūnebrēs'
Stage 16	'rēx spectāculum dat'

Stage commentaries

The various suggestions for questions, further work etc. in the stage commentaries are intended as a 'bank' on which teachers may draw or not, as they think fit.

Books are normally referred to by the name of their author. For details of title, publisher, etc., see Bibliography, pp.43ff.

A list of the linguistic features introduced and discussed in each stage is given in the 'Linguistic synopsis of Unit IIA' on pp.37–8.

STAGE 13: IN BRITANNIĀ

Synopsis

Reading passages ⎫ ⎧ Gaius Salvius Liberalis
Background material ⎭ ⎩ farming and slavery in Roman Britain

Main language features   infinitive with present tense of *volō* and *possum*
-que

Model sentences

Gaius Salvius Liberalis is the central character of the stages that deal with Roman Britain (13–16) and he will reappear in Unit IIIA. The model sentences introduce him and his household, together with the new linguistic feature: the infinitive with the present tense of *volō* and *possum*.

For suggestions about presenting and handling the model sentences, see Handbook to Unit I, p.16.

Many pupils find it easier initially to translate *potest* by 'is able to' rather than the generally more idiomatic 'can', especially as the infinitive is new, but by the end of this stage pupils should be expected to handle both translations, which are featured in the first language note, pp.10–11.

The teacher might briefly invite comment on the nationality of some of the slaves: Varica (British but Romanised), Philus (Greek and educated), Volubilis (Egyptian: notice the eyes) and Bregans (British and unromanised). Their jobs, largely the result of their nationality and education, can be discussed here too.

Pupils may be intrigued by Philus' abacus, the ancient equivalent of their own calculators. The counting-board, with its beads and columns for units, tens, hundreds etc. (or monetary equivalents), may strike them as unsophisticated, but the abacus is still widely used in some parts of the world, notably Japan and Russia.

The following words are new: *cūrat* (new meaning), *potest, fessus, vult, vōcem, suāvem, agilis, saltāre, geminī, nōlunt.*

trēs servī

For suggestions on handling the reading passages, see Unit I Handbook, pp.18–23.

This passage is suitable for reading aloud by pupils. The atmosphere is one of grumbling and discontent among the slaves; encourage the pupils to convey this in their reading, together with the abrupt change of mood on the arrival of Varica and his news. Pupils could perhaps be asked what they would have thought about going to Britain had they been a slave like Philus or Volubilis; the differences between them and the Briton Bregans will be amplified in 'Bregāns' and 'Salvius fundum īnspicit'. The class might also be asked to find in the text the probable answer to Volubilis' second question.

The past participle *vulnerātus* and the neuter nominative singular *vīnum* do not require special comment; participles can be treated as adjectives until they are formally discussed in the language notes of Stages 20–22, and the neuter singular dealt with in Unit IIB.

Pupils rarely have trouble with *nōlō* (line 9) when translating from Latin; it can simply be pointed out that *nōlō* equals *nōn volō*.

The new format of the vocabularies at the end of each story should be discussed. Verbs are listed as they occur in the story, followed by their infinitive and meaning; nouns as they occur, followed by their nominative singular and meaning.

coniūrātiō

The title is worth discussing with pupils after reading the story. It is somewhat ironical, because the 'conspiracy' (although described as such by Varica) exists only in Salvius' imagination. Pupils may point out that the guards were clearly not involved in the plot because they came in and killed Alator before he had a chance to murder Salvius.

The story is an introduction to Salvius' character and also introduces new aspects of slavery. The important distinction should be made between the generally humane treatment of slaves (especially if educated) in the *familia urbāna*, and conditions in the *familia rūstica* where slaves were often regarded as animals and worked in chain gangs (see the picture, pupil's text p.7; and filmstrip 21, slide 41). Life for the slaves in the mines was particularly bad; many died through overwork or flogging. 'Death in their eyes is more to be desired than life, because of the magnitude of the hardships they must bear.' (Diodorus V.38; for fuller quotation see Lewis and Reinhold II.158.)

It was in fact illegal at this time to execute a slave without trial before a magistrate (for legislation on slaves see Lewis and Reinhold II.268–70); but, as the story implies, the law could be ignored, especially by a person of Salvius' authority, in a province remote from Rome. What we would regard as cruelty to slaves was not uncommon. Like Salvius, Cato (writing *c.*160 B.C.) recommends reducing the rations of sick slaves (*De Agri Cultura* II.4). The mass execution initially demanded by Salvius recalls Tacitus' description of the execution of over four hundred slaves of Pedanius Secundus just over twenty years previously (*Annals* XIV.42–5), where treatment of slaves becomes a matter of debate, and the murder of Larcius Macedo by his slaves and their punishment. Parts of either story could be read to pupils in translation (both are in Lewis and Reinhold II.265–6; see also C.S.C.P. *The Roman World* Unit II Item 16b (Tacitus) and Pliny tr. Greig p.23. It should be made clear that both cases are unusual: mass execution of slaves was legal, but the law rarely seems to have been applied. As time went on, treatment of slaves generally became more humane.

The class might be asked how they think the slaves would react (*a*) to the story of Salvius' injury, (*b*) to the prospect of Salvius' imminent arrival.

(Note that the Cantici are frequently found in books on Roman Britain as the Cantiaci or Cantii.)

Bregāns

After the teacher has read it aloud, part or all of this story could be studied by pupils on their own or in groups. The whole class could then look at the questions together. The passage is also suitable for presentation as a play. (Characters needed: narrator, Varica, Loquax, Anti-Loquax, Bregans, Salvius. Other members of the class can play non-speaking roles as horsemen and slaves.)

Pupils sometimes translate *ancillae dominō nostrō cubiculum parant* (line 8) as 'The slave-girls are preparing our master's bedroom.' As they have not yet met the genitive, it is probably best to say that this is nearly but not quite right and remind them of how they translated *Metella fīliō dōnum quaerēbat* (model sentences, Stage 9) or *ego omnibus supplicium poscō* ('coniūrātiō' line 20).

The story can be used for practising the 1st and 2nd persons of the imperfect (introduced in Stage 12) by means of a substitution exercise of the kind described in Unit I Teacher's Handbook p.24, in which pupils are asked to translate (e.g.) *stābant* in line 20, then to say what *stābāmus* or *stābās* would mean. The story also contains a number of sentences or part-sentences with no subject stated (e.g. *vīlicus per ōrdinēs ambulābat; servōs īnspiciēbat et numerābat* (lines 5–6)). These could be practised orally, or listed to form a written exercise. It may be advisable to include the previous sentence or part-sentence, if the subject is expressed there.

Question 6 raises the problem of Bregans' character: the story shows him clamouring like a child for attention but brave enough (or stupid enough) to answer back to Salvius at the end.

The dog was probably of a breed similar to a modern Irish Wolfhound. British hunting dogs were highly prized in the empire and a major export. For details of hunting, see Birley 91–2 and Balsdon 219–20. A picture of a British hunting dog appears in the pupil's text, p.9.

First language note (infinitive + volō/possum)

After the language note has been read and studied, the class should look back at one or more of the stories they have read so far, and pick out and translate sentences containing infinitives. For further practice, questions in Latin might be asked, for example on 'trēs servī' the teacher might ask, *'quis ad Ītaliam redīre vult?'*, *'quis dormīre vult?'*, etc. Similar questions could then be asked on the model sentences; then, to practise the 1st person singular the class itself could be asked *'quis saltāre potest?'*, *'quis cantāre potest?'*, *'quis dormīre vult?'* and so on, inviting the reply *'ego saltāre possum'*, etc. (This sort of questioning can usefully fill the odd minute or two at the end of a lesson.)

By the end of Stage 13, pupils should be confident about translating *possum* as 'I can' as well as 'I am able' – this can be practised by requiring both versions when translating the examples in the language note. As a further exercise, these could be transferred from singular to plural or vice versa.

Salvius fundum īnspicit

A tour of Salvius' farm, based on Cato's advice to a landowner about an inspection of his farm with the bailiff or foreman (Cato, *De Agri Cultura* II; Lewis and Reinhold I.443). Pupils could first read the story by themselves either for homework or in class in groups or pairs. The teacher might then read the passage through and ask comprehension questions, for example:
  What did Salvius want to do?

Who took him over the farm?

What did Varica say about the harvest?

Where was the grain stored?

What was the name of the slave in charge of the ploughmen?

Why was he absent?

What was the effect of his absence?

When Salvius proposed to get rid of him, what did Varica say on his behalf?

Why did Salvius grudge the ploughmen their food?

What did Salvius see next to the granary?

Why was it half-ruined?

Was there any special reason why Salvius regarded Bregans as *stultior quam cēterī?*

What impression do you get of Salvius as an estate owner?

This will probably lead into a discussion of Salvius. Pupils will again notice his hard and unsympathetic features, but the teacher should draw them away from seeing him as a mere stereotype of villainy. He is more complex than that. He is shown here in the role of an estate owner who, though he employs a bailiff for day-to-day supervision, takes a direct personal interest in its management. He comes in person to see that the estate is being run efficiently and economically. He views the slaves impersonally as one factor in the economics of a profitable business, and in so doing he behaves in a way that would be regarded as normal and acceptable by many Romans. (Some pupils may widen the moral issue by saying that in that case there was something wrong with the Romans' own standards.)

Varica's behaviour may also be explored. In Salvius' absence he takes charge and shows himself capable of making decisions and organising the work. Now that Salvius has come and is demanding an account of his management, his attitude is somewhat diffident, even obsequious. For further details of the job of a vilicus and farming generally, see C.S.C.P. *The Roman World* Unit II Book 7 *The Villa*, Lewis and Reinhold I.440–50, II.167–75, Birley 78–99. For further information on villas generally, see Percival. See filmstrip 5–6; Unit III slides 34–5.

For further work, pupils could make a list of the slaves who belonged to Salvius, with their duties. They could perhaps work out the chain of command (Salvius → Varica → Cervix → Bregans and the others) and comparisons could be made with the specialised division of labour of servants in a wealthy Victorian family. Salvius' attitude to his slaves could also be further discussed and compared with Caecilius' in Unit I (see especially Stage 6). Pupils should look out for differences in treatment of individual slaves. In Stage 14, the focus will shift from the farm slaves to the domestic staff.

Second language note (-que)

-*que* is often forgotten; it may be helpful to make up some further easy
sentences containing *et* and ask pupils to replace *et* by -*que* in the right
position. This exercise could use vocabulary from the 'Words and phrases
checklist' and be done immediately before the pupils study the list for
homework.

Manipulation exercises

Exercise 1   Type: completion
Missing item: infinitive
Criterion of choice: sense

Exercise 2   Type: completion
Missing item: verb
Criterion of choice: sense and morphology
Linguistic feature being practised: 1st, 2nd and 3rd persons
singular of perfect, introduced in Stages 6 and 12
Incidental practice: clauses with *quod*

This exercise should be taken orally in the first instance and followed if
necessary by further practice in discriminating the singular forms of the
perfect tense.

In completion exercises done orally, it is always worth insisting that
pupils answer in full sentences.

The background material

This should be split up. The material on Salvius can be dealt with at any
time during the stage; that on farming and villas fits best with 'Salvius
fundum īnspicit' and that on slavery with 'coniūrātiō'.

Salvius

Gaius Salvius Liberalis Nonius Bassus came from the city of Salvia in the
Picenum region of central Italy. Although he may have spent little time
there as an adult, he maintained his connections with Salvia by acting as
its *patrōnus*.

After making a successful start to his legal career and entering the
Senate, he became at a surprisingly early age a member of the Fratres
Arvales, who were usually all drawn from senatorial families of long
standing and had close contact with the emperor, who was always a
member. Salvius was clearly destined for power. He also held the post of

lēgātus legiōnis in Moesia with the Fifth Legion Macedonica before coming to Britain.

His duties as *iūridīcus* may have included comparing British and Roman laws and working out a new legal code for use by the governors in their edicts and it is possible that he had a special commission to take over the administration of the kingdom of Cogidubnus after the king's death and incorporate it into the imperial estates.

We have imagined the home of Salvius in Britain as being Angmering near Worthing in Sussex, where excavations, unfortunately now covered up, have revealed a villa, unusually elaborate for the first century. Its craftsmanship and planning are surpassed, in the early years of the Roman occupation, only by the magnificence of the nearby palace of Fishbourne.

It seems that Salvius received a consulship and returned to Rome by 87, but like many protégés of Vespasian, he soon fell foul of Domitian and went into exile. We next see him in 100 under Trajan defending the provincial governor Priscus. Pliny, in his account of the case (*Letters* II.11.17), describes him as an acute, methodical, spirited and eloquent orator. He also seems to have been outspoken. Vespasian earlier had commended him for saying, while defending a rich client, 'What is it to Caesar if Hipparchus has a hundred millions?' (Suetonius, *Life of Vespasian* 13) in reply to the unspoken suggestion that Vespasian might wish to have Hipparchus condemned unjustly in order to seize his vast wealth.

Although Salvius had clearly resumed his legal career in Rome, he does not appear to have returned to political life, and when offered the governorship of Asia, he declined for reasons unknown.

His full career is outlined in *C.I.L.* IX.5533; Dessau 1011. With the abbreviations expanded the inscription reads as follows:

> *Gaio Salvio, Gaii filio, Velia, Liberali Nonio Basso, consuli, proconsuli provinciae Macedoniae, legato Augustorum, iuridico Britanniae, legato legionis V Macedonicae, fratri Arvali, allecto ab divo Vespasiano et divo Tito inter tribunicios, ab isdem allecto inter praetorios, quinquennali IIII, patrono coloniae. hic sorte proconsul factus provinciae Asiae se excusavit.*

To Gaius Salvius Liberalis Nonius Bassus, son of Gaius, of the Velian (voting-tribe), consul, proconsul of the province of Macedonia, imperial legate, chief justice of Britain, legate of the Fifth Legion Macedonica, Arval Brother, promoted to the tribunate by the divine Vespasian and the divine Titus and promoted by the same to the praetorship, a municipal magistrate for twenty years and patron of his town. He obtained by lot the proconsulship of Asia, but excused himself from it.

The gravestone mentioning Rufilla is Dessau 1012. Expanded version:

Vitelliae Gaii filiae Rufillae Gaii Salvi Liberalis consulis, flamini Salutis Augusti, matri optumae, Gaius Salvius Vitellianus vivos.

To Vitellia Rufilla, daughter of Gaius, (the wife) of Gaius Salvius Liberalis the consul, priestess of the welfare of the emperor, best of mothers, Gaius Salvius Vitellianus (set this up) in his lifetime.

It is not necessary to deal with Salvius' career in too much detail here, as he will appear again in Unit IIIA, but it is useful for pupils to know the outline of his life up to his posting to Britain. At this point they should be encouraged to build up a picture of a man in authority, whose character betrays the ruthlessness of a successful politician and the arrogance of a *novus homō*. These traits are particularly evident in his dealings with the provincials. But the picture ought not to be too one-sided. The unscrupulousness which pupils recognise and condemn in him needs to be balanced against other considerations, and pupils should be encouraged to think of reasons for his behaviour. A man in Salvius' position and with his responsibilities might be motivated by genuine fear of a slave-uprising or by fear of the emperor or of the powerful imperial freedmen. In answering to the emperor for his actions Salvius would be judged less by moral standards than his success or failure. In order to encourage them to see both sides of the argument, pupils could perhaps at the end of Stage 13 write and act out a conversation between a friend and an enemy of Salvius based on all that they have read.

Farming in Roman Britain

The villa, see under 'Salvius fundum īnspicit', p.8 above.

The picture on p.16 of the pupil's text is an aerial photograph. Pupils need to realise that the site is not excavated and that the markings, caused by the disturbance of the earth, are only visible from the air and only under certain conditions. Help them to trace the outermost lines of the boundary and the subdivisions of the fields; once they have grasped the scale they may be able to identify the outline of the villa buildings towards the left-hand corner of the site.

The slaves, see under 'coniūrātiō', p.6 above.

Words and phrases checklist

The new format of these lists should be explained to pupils and compared with that of the story vocabularies (see note, p.5 above). 1st and 2nd declension nouns are listed under their nominative singular, 3rd declension nouns by nominative and accusative singular. Verbs are listed by their first three principal parts. Before going on to Stage 14, pupils should be expected to be able to recognise these: it may be helpful to do some oral work on parts derived from them; see suggestions in Unit I Teacher's Handbook, pp.25–6.

Suggestions for further work

1 Pupils might be encouraged to do a project on local Roman villas or Celtic settlements. The local museum and archaeological society may be able to supply helpful information. If there is a Roman or Romano-British site near the school, it would be useful to preface a visit by inviting a local expert to give a short talk about the techniques of excavation and the way that archaeological evidence can be interpreted to shed light on the development and uses of the site. This aspect can be developed when the background material on Romano-British archaeology is read in the final stage of Unit IIIA. Pupils may also be interested to know when the Romans came to their particular area and how life changed as a result.

2 At this stage, pupils might enjoy writing imaginatively about slavery. This might take the form of a story about a slave in the mines or a play, perhaps written and acted by a group, based on normal living conditions on a villa estate. The tradition of slaves trying to outwit their masters in Roman comedy could be mentioned here. Tranio is a good example, and any previous reading from the *Mostellaria* in translation (see Unit I Teacher's Handbook p.49) could be recalled at this point.

3 A wide range of archaeological material on Roman Britain for teachers and pupils is available from a University of Sheffield service. There are teaching packs, slide packs, artifact kits, replicas and video tapes. Of special interest for this Unit are the teaching pack and slide pack on Roman Britain, the Roman villa artifact kit and video tape 2 on the Roman countryside (excavating and reconstructing a villa estate). The items are reasonably priced, with reduced rates for subscribers, to whom some items are restricted. Write to: Archaeology in Education, Department of Prehistory and Archaeology, University of Sheffield, Sheffield S10 2TN.

STAGE 14: APUD SALVIUM

Synopsis

Reading passages	daily life in Salvius' villa
Background material	life in Roman Britain (general and historical survey)
Main language features	agreement of adjective (case and number) imperfect of *possum*

N.B. This stage is rather long and it is important not to get 'bogged down'. It is suggested that some stories are done quickly (e.g. 'Rūfilla cubiculum ōrnat', 'Quīntus advenit') or omitted and summarised.

Title page

Pupils may need help with the translation of the title page; they have only met *apud* so far in the phrase *apud Canticōs*. If they have met *chez* in French, the new meaning of *apud* could be emphasised by asking them the French for *apud mē*.

Model sentences

These contain a further development of the infinitive: its use with sentences such as *difficile est mihi, necesse est mihi*, etc. Most pupils absorb this new use comfortably and it will probably not need comment from the teacher: if the pupils experience difficulty either in the model sentences or in the reading passages, the easiest solution is to give them further examples, e.g.

> *difficile est Philō magnam amphoram portāre, quod senex est.*
> *necesse est Bregantī amphorās gravēs portāre.*
> *necesse est vōbīs dīligenter labōrāre.*
> *difficile est mihi librum portāre.*

This use of the infinitive will be revised in the second language note of Stage 16, together with other uses, such as infinitive with *dēbeō*, etc.

The model sentences also give practice in a feature which has been present in the material since Stage 3, but not discussed until this stage – the agreement of noun and attributive adjective in case and number. It is suggested that this aspect of the model sentences should be left undiscussed on first reading, but that the class return to them later, after reading the two language notes, to study the examples of agreement here (see below under 'Second language note').

Pupils will probably identify with Bregans here and cast parents and teachers in the role of Varica. It might be worthwhile to discuss with pupils the causes of Bregans' (and their own) attitudes.

The following words are new: *gravis, necesse.*

Rūfilla

A fairly easy passage, which could be done as a play (Filmstrip 18 will help to set the scene, or C.S.C.P. *The Roman World* Unit I Item 22). Rufilla is stereotyped here as the nagging wife, but it is worth reminding pupils of the considerable standing of a *mātrōna Rōmāna,* who had the task of supervising a large domestic staff. For the evidence on Rufilla, see Stage 13 p.15 and this Handbook, p.11 above. It is important for the class to understand that Salvius' remarks from *'Semprōnia, amīca mea. . .'* to *'. . . mihi nihil dās'* are his report of earlier speeches by Rufilla.

Pupils might be asked why Rufilla sends her hairdressers out of the room before arguing with her husband.

The infinitives could be picked out and practised and some stress perhaps placed on *cotīdiē* (often forgotten) and *nōnne* with its variety of translations. (*nōnne* will appear in the second language note of Stage 15.)

The evidence for Roman London at this time is not plentiful, but it seems probable that it was the administrative centre for Britain and is therefore Salvius' likely base. As a port it would be closer than the rest of the country to the Roman culture which Rufilla seems to miss. Life there would certainly be more lively than at a *vīlla rūstica,* like Angmering.

Several of the domestic slaves are named or referred to in this and the following stories; their varied tasks and status might be noted in passing.

Domitilla cubiculum parat

A story which works best if taken quickly. Subsequent discussion might focus on the character of Domitilla: her petulance, her consciousness of her status as an *ōrnātrīx* and her ability to manipulate Volubilis the cook.

Again there are plenty of infinitives which can be picked out and translated. Sentences of the type *necesse est nōbīs cubiculum parāre* (line 4) are also useful for practising the dative. Pupils can be asked to list the datives, or change the person involved, e.g. 'What would *necesse est vōbīs cubiculum parāre* mean?' or, using the Language Information pamphlet, 'What would be the Latin for "It is necessary for the slaves to prepare the bedroom"?'

This story also contains the first example of *nōlī* + infinitive. The literal translation could be supplied if pupils ask about it, but fuller discussion should be postponed until the language note in Stage 19.

Pupils might be invited to comment on the title; its irony is usually appreciated.

First language note (adjective agreement of case and number)

Agreement of the adjective is discussed in three steps. The present language note deals with case and number where noun and adjective have similar endings. The next language note introduces examples with dissimilar endings and a language note in Stage 18 deals with gender. It is recommended that teachers stick to this step-by-step approach and do not try to anticipate; it is safer to teach one step thoroughly than to risk confusion by teaching two steps together.

In paragraphs 3 and 5 it is often helpful to replace the general instruction 'Find the noun described by each adjective' with a specific question '*Who* was frightened?', '*Who* was small?', etc. This presents the noun-adjective relationship in terms of meaning rather than as an abstraction.

After the language note has been studied, pupils should be asked to pick out adjectives from stories already read and state the noun each describes. It will be necessary for the time being to restrict examples to nouns and adjectives of the same declension.

Rūfilla cubiculum ōrnat

This story develops the characters of Rufilla and Domitilla (pupils might be asked if they think the latter's suggestion is intended to be helpful or to make mischief). It also provides some useful practice on the endings of the perfect tense, whose 1st and 2nd persons were introduced in Stage 12. Examples of the perfect could first be listed on the board and then questions asked such as 'What is the difference in meaning between *optimē labōrāvistī* (line 9) and *bene labōrāvistis* (line 15)?' and 'If *Domitillam cōnspexit* (line 3) means "She caught sight of Domitilla" what would *Domitillam cōnspexī* mean?' and 'What would the Latin be for "We caught sight of Domitilla"?'. And so on.

Second language note (adjective agreement with different endings)

Study of this note can be followed by identifying the case and number of noun and adjective pairs in section 3 and then by going back to the model sentences (pp.22–3) and picking out the adjectives, saying which nouns they are describing and doing some more identification of case and number. Similar practice can be based on the stories. For treatment of adjectives generally, see under 'First language note' above.

in tablīnō

Some of the questions attached to this passage go beyond surface comprehension into points of interpretation and character. It will probably be necessary to run through the translation first.

A light-hearted but useful lead-in to discussion of character is often to ask pupils to 'cast' characters by using well-known television personalities – many comedies have a couple to match Rufilla and Salvius. Salvius is of course annoyed (question 3) by the interruption of his session with Philus *and* the loss of his furniture. He therefore has little patience with Rufilla's announcement that a visitor will shortly arrive. Her efforts to explain that he is a person of respectable social standing who escaped from the destruction of Pompeii merely provoke an outburst of prejudice against untrustworthy Pompeian merchants. Rufilla, incidentally, exaggerates when she says '*Quīntus vir nōbilis est*' (line 25–6). Quintus' grandfather was a slave and any noble connections he may have come from Rufilla's side of the family.

aliquid (lines 7 and 15) might deserve special comment: pupils often forget it. It recurs in 'tripodes argenteī'. *num* (line 33) is also worth revising. It occurred first in Stage 11 (see second language note there) and will recur in the second language note of Stage 15.

Manipulation exercises

Exercise 1   Type: translation
Linguistic feature being practised: infinitive

Exercise 2   Type: completion
Missing item: noun
Criterion of choice: sense and morphology
Linguistic feature being practised: nominative and accusative
singular and plural, introduced in Stages 2, 5 and 8

In this exercise, choice of correct noun guarantees the correct choice between singular and plural, but a further choice has to be made between nominative and accusative.

Quīntus advenit

The much-heralded appearance of Quintus usually arouses varied reactions in pupils; the reason for his arrival in Britain is not revealed for the moment. The class may be surprised to find Salvius being polite – even if his politeness is superficial – and it is perhaps worth reminding pupils that Quintus is the first Roman citizen with whom we have seen Salvius dealing. The etiquette of hospitality was strict in the ancient world and Salvius, though he speaks ironically, has no difficulty in controlling his feelings.

Pupils may need help with the perfect form *rīsit* and this may be a useful place to revise the perfect tense. Practice could be given in the use of the 'Words and phrases' section of the Language Information pamphlet to look up perfect forms such as *discessī, cēpimus, posuistī,* etc.

tripodes argenteī

This story motivates the journey to Cogidubnus' palace in Stage 15 and can be read fairly quickly. Pupils might be asked to do the first reading of the passage on their own or in groups. This could be followed by comprehension questions rather than translation, e.g.

> What were the slaves doing?
> Who came into the bedroom to speak to Quintus?
> What message did he bring?
> What gift did Quintus extract from his box and for whom was it intended?
> What did Salvius say when told of Quintus' choice of gift?
> Why do you think Salvius said 'no' to his steward's first two suggestions?
> Why did the steward discourage Salvius from taking the *statua aurāta*?
> Suggest a suitable translation for the last sentence.
> Do you think Salvius had intended to take a present at all to Cogidubnus?
> What reasons do you think Quintus had for offering a present to the king?

The scale of value of the articles made in various metals could be discussed. Cheapest is *aēneus* (made of bronze) – which even Salvius rejects. Then comes *argenteus* (made of silver) – Quintus' tripods. At the top would come *aureus* (made of gold). Salvius' cleverness – or meanness – lies in his suggestion of taking something *aurātus* (gold-plated), which appears the best, but is in fact of very little value. The mention of imported wine and valuable articles in this story can lead to preliminary discussion about the movement of goods in the Roman empire, based on the background material. Further work can be done on this later in connection with the background material and map in Stage 17.

If pupils are unclear what a tripod is, they should be referred to the picture, which shows the two *tripodes argenteī* together with the *urna aēnea*.

Third language note (imperfect of possum)

Pupils are unlikely to have much difficulty over this note. For further practice for able pupils the teacher could give some simple sentences containing imperfects for pupils to turn into infinitive + imperfect of *possum* (using 'Words and phrases' to find the infinitive), e.g.

servus nōn currēbat.   This becomes: *servus currere nōn poterat.*

ego nōn labōrābam.   This becomes: *ego labōrāre nōn poteram.*

The pupils should translate both sentences.

Further examples:

servus amphoram nōn portābat.
tū nōn dormiēbās.
ancillae nōn saltābant.
vōs servōs nōn vidēbātis.
nōs nōn currēbāmus.

The background material

This can be studied and discussed at any convenient point during the stage.

Pupils can be asked to identify the towns marked on the map on p.37 of the pupil's text and consider their significance for the Romans. The location of minerals will provide a clue to discussion of question 1 below, in conjunction with other information in the material.

The inscription from Claudius' arch (C.I.L. 920), pupil's text p.38. This is the most substantial part of the inscribed stone. Three small fragments, found in the same place, are assumed to belong to the same inscription, and have enabled scholars to make the following conjectural reconstruction.

[ ] = missing part of stone; ( ) = expansion of abbreviation.

TI(BERIO) CLAV[DIO DRVSI F(ILIO) CAI]SARI
AVGV[STO GERMANI]CO
PONTIFIC[I MAXIMO TRIB(VNICIA) POTES]TAT(E) XI
COS(VL) V IM[PERATORI XII PATRI PA]TRIAI
SENATVS PO[PVLVSQVE] RO[MANVS Q]VOD
REGES BRIT[ANNIAE] XI [DEVICTOS SINE]
VLLA IACTV[RA IN DEDITIONEM ACCEPERIT]
GENTESQVE B[ARBARAS TRANS OCEANVM]
PRIMVS IN DICI[ONEM POPVLI ROMANI REDEGERIT]

To the Emperor Tiberius Claudius, son of Drusus, Caesar Augustus
Germanicus, Pontifex Maximus, holding tribunician power for the
eleventh time, Consul for the fifth time, saluted as *Imperator* twenty-two
times, Censor, Father of his Country. The Senate and people of Rome
(set this up), because he received the surrender of eleven British
kings, who were defeated without any loss, and because he was the first
to bring barbarian peoples on the other side of the Ocean under
Roman rule.

The 'eleven kings' probably included Cogidubnus. See Frere pp.82ff.

The picture on p.40 of the pupil's text shows the Roman road on
Wheeldale Moor. The foundation of the road is visible, raised to form a
camber (there were drainage culverts at intervals). Originally the large
stones would have been covered first with a layer of gravel and then with
a smooth surface of smaller stones.

Suggestions for discussion

1 Why did the Romans want to invade Britain?
2 By what methods, military and otherwise, did they succeed?
3 Why did they find Britain difficult to conquer?
4 What advantages and disadvantages were there in living within the
Roman empire?

For further information on topics mentioned in the background
material, see:
Caesar's invasion: *Gallic War* IV.23 – V.23. Includes a description of the
    Celtic inhabitants and vague information about geography and
    resources, which is worth reading to pupils to give an idea of Roman
    myths and prejudices about Britain. Compare Strabo, *Geography*
    IV.5.2 and 4. See also Webster, *Boudica* pp.34–6.
Claudius' invasion: Lewis and Reinhold II.112–13 (from Dio Cassius
    LX.19–22.1). See also Frere, ch.4 and 5; Webster, *The Roman Invasion
    of Britain*. Leonard Cottrell, *The Great Invasion* can be given to bright
    pupils.
Caratacus: Tacitus, *Annals* XII.33–40. See also Webster, *Rome against
    Caratacus*.
Boudica: Dio Cassius LXII.1–12, Tacitus, *Annals* XIV.31–7. See also
    Dudley and Webster; Webster, *Boudica*; Andrews. (Boudica is the
    spelling generally preferred by modern scholars.)
Extracts from most of the sources mentioned above, dealing with the
    early conquest, can be found in translation in C.S.C.P. *The Romans
    discover Britain*.

For further reading on Roman Britain, see Bibliography, pp.43–6. For pictures see filmstrip title frame and 1–3; slides 52–3.

Suggestions for further work

1 Supply the class with information about Boudica's rebellion in A.D. 61 and perhaps Caesar's description of the Britons (see above). They could then write an imaginative account of the destruction of a farmstead or the diary of a Roman officer sent against Boudica, with observations about the British and how they fight.

2 Pupils could be encouraged to collect material for a wall display on Roman Britain – newspaper cuttings, magazine articles, etc. These can be added to and changed over the weeks spent on Unit IIA and later used or referred to in Unit IIIA.

3 Map work: it would be useful to have maps of Britain available to show mountains and rivers (as an explanation of why the Roman tactics developed as they did), major cities and forts, British tribes, major Roman roads, major mineral deposits, etc. The pupils could either draw their own or produce large ones for display, perhaps using an outline map provided by the teacher. They should be encouraged to provide scale, key and title. For geographical information on Roman Britain use the map produced by the Ordnance Survey.

4 Pupils with an interest in model soldiers may enjoy re-living the invasions by moving their troops over a large map or model of southern England, as one of the accounts (see above) is read to them.

STAGE 15: RĒX COGIDUBNUS

Synopsis

Reading passages } { King Cogidubnus
Background material }   { the palace at Fishbourne

Main language features   relative clause
nōnne?

Model sentences

These introduce Cogidubnus in person. For details of Cogidubnus, see below, pp.25ff.

The sentence pattern nominative + accusative + verb is now expanded by the addition of a relative clause. The sentences should first be read aloud by the teacher, with appropriate pauses and word grouping. Pupils rarely have difficulty in translating the relative pronoun in these contexts, especially if they have done French and make the association with *qui* and *que*. If they get stuck, they should be referred to the pictures and contextual clues. If passive translations are produced, (e.g. 'The wine, which was being carried by the slave-girls, . . .'), a helpful way to correct this is to write *ancillae vīnum ferēbant* on the board and to ask for a translation of that, and then go back to the model sentences and ask for a re-translation.

Detailed discussion of relative clauses should wait until pupils have had plenty of experience of them – there is a language note later in the stage. Unless the pupils mention it, there is no need to comment here on the double meaning of *quod*.

Pupils may need help on a number of technical terms here (e.g. *patera, lībāvit, āra, sacerdōs)* and may want to discuss animal sacrifices.

The following words are new: *scēptrum, diadēma, rēgīna, maximē, patera, agnum, āram, victima, sacerdōs, bālāvit.*

ad aulam

After the first reading, the first paragraph could be revised by asking the pupils to make a rough sketch of the procession in their books (using stick men or similar); or successive pupils might be asked to draw the various items in the procession on the blackboard as they are reached in the text, thus building up a frieze.

The *dignitās* of Salvius is revealed in the manner of his journey to the palace. His retinue is preceded by slaves who act as *praecursōrēs* and are responsible for clearing any obstructions. The number of his attendants, the gifts they carry and the fine horses ridden by Salvius and Quintus are all calculated to impress upon observers his rank, wealth and importance; pupils could be asked to supply modern comparisons. Salvius' contemptuous attitude to the provincials, evident earlier in his treatment of Bregans and the Cantican miners, is here seen extended to those who, like the young men with the wagon, are not his slaves. The truth or otherwise of his final remark could be discussed.

The first two paragraphs contain a number of examples of the imperfect tense. For revision in the few minutes remaining before the end of a lesson, questions might be asked to practise the different persons of the imperfect. For example:

What did *servus tripodas portābat* (line 5) mean?
What would *servī tripodas portābant* mean?

And *tripodas portābant?*

And *tripodas portābam?*

Or:

Look at the first sentence. What did it mean?

Now what would the Latin be for 'Quintus was proceeding'?

And 'Quintus was proceeding to the hall with many slaves'?

And 'We were proceeding'?

And so on. The Language Information pamphlet, p.8, should be referred to as and when necessary.

The imperfect of *esse* could also be revised, e.g.

What did *magna turba erat in viā* (line 9) mean?

What would *erant in viā* mean?

And *in viā erāmus?*

What would be the Latin for 'I was in the road'?

caerimōnia

This is an imagined ceremony at which Cogidubnus annually honours the memory of the Emperor Claudius. It is based on a description by Herodian (*History* IV.2, Lewis and Reinhold II.565–6) of the ritual that marked the apotheosis of an emperor after his death. This is of course a Roman, not a British, ritual and Cogidubnus, now an old man, sticks to it with the tenacity of a convert to a new cult. He is dignified and respected, but now lame and living on his memories of the past. He does not recognise that with the coming of Salvius his old position and prestige are almost ended.

The word 'pyre' may require explanation by the teacher or (preferably) a member of the class. The eagle is used as a symbol of Roman power and the magical effect is designed to impress a gullible and superstitious audience of Britons – and even Romans, who liked such tricks at their dinner parties (see note on Stage 16 model sentences).

Consolidation work might concentrate on verbs. Pupils could practise the present, imperfect and perfect tenses in a substitution exercise of the kind described in Unit I Teacher's Handbook, p.24. Ask such questions as:

In line 30, what did *in āreā erat rogus* mean?

What would *in āreā est rogus* mean?

What did *prīncipēs ad rogum cum magnā dignitāte prōcessērunt* mean?

What would *prīncipēs ad rogum cum magnā dignitāte prōcēdunt* mean?

And for able pupils, using the Language Information pamphlet:

What would be the Latin for 'The chieftains were proceeding to the pyre with great dignity'?

Encourage pupils to reply in complete Latin sentences, in order to

prove their pronunciation and grasp of sentence-structure. Revision of
e different forms the perfect tense can take would be appropriate here,
efore the introduction of the pluperfect in Stage 16. It is worth practising
me examples of those verbs (such as *ascendit* (line 37), *dēscendit, ruit,
ntendit)* whose 3rd singular perfect and present are the same.

idī fūnebrēs

his boat race is based on Virgil's account of the funeral games
elebrated in honour of Anchises (*Aeneid* V.114–285). Virgil's games are
erived in turn from Homeric funeral games. The boat-race, however, is a
oman rather than a Greek feature.

Funeral games may need to be explained. They would normally be a
spectful but cheerful event in honour of the dead, following a period of
ourning; the games in this story mark the anniversary of the emperor's
eath and have political as well as religious overtones.

This story needs planning if it is to succeed. It is long and quite
ifficult, particularly because it contains a lot of new vocabulary, but the
arrative has much more impact if taken at one sitting. If there is a
ouble period available, use it for this story if possible; if not, something
ke the following approach could be tried.

Start off by reading short portions of text aloud and asking simple
mprehension questions such as:

Who led the procession to the sea-shore?

When?

What did the Britons do there?

Which tribes were present?

ranslation need not be attempted at this stage. Comprehension
uestions could cover the story-line up to *hoc saxum erat mēta* (line 22).

At this point the teacher could draw on the blackboard a sketch plan of
e shore, spectators and turning-point, using white chalk. Then one
upil could be asked to come up to the front with his book and given a
iece of blue chalk for Belimicus' boat and another pupil a yellow piece
r Dumnorix'. A little table on the blackboard, built up from pupils'
nswers to comprehension questions, is often useful for reference:

blue	*yellow*
Belimicus	Dumnorix
Cantici	Regnenses

The rest of the story could be translated rapidly by the class working
ogether, assisted where necessary by the teacher, and the progress of the
wo boats can meanwhile be marked on the board by the pupils.

For homework pupils could translate part or all of the first half of the
tory, which was only covered by comprehension questions before. The

following lesson this translation could be gone over in class and discussed. Idiomatic translations of *in amīcitiā* (line 3), e.g. 'friendly with', 'on friendly terms with', should be encouraged. A fair copy of some or all of the homework could be made and the rest of the story run through.

Encourage pupils to observe the rivalry between the two Celtic chieftains, echoed by their oarsmen and their tribal supporters watching on the shore. Dumnorix and Belimicus have a touchy sense of personal honour; they are quick to mock and take offence. Attention could be drawn to the differences in character and skills between Belimicus and Dumnorix and to Belimicus' final humiliation. Do we have any sympathy for him? The reaction of the spectators may also be mentioned and comparisons may be made with modern forms of crowd behaviour.

laetissimī (line 4), *rōbustissimus* (line 6), *perītissimus* (line 10) and possibly *optimam* (line 20) could lead to a brief revision of superlative adjectives, and *stultior* (line 21) of comparatives. Comparative adverbs (e.g. *celerius* (line 5)) need not be mentioned yet unless asked about by pupils.

Rēgnēnsēs laetī, Canticī miserī erant (lines 44–5) is the first example of a sentence where the first of two verbs is suppressed. It needs no special comment here; if help is needed, comprehension questions should suffice. There will be more examples in Unit IIB and this sentence pattern is commented on in Unit IIB Language Information pamphlet, p.22.

Treatment of this story could perhaps end with a reading of the *Aeneid* boat-race in translation and then the class could move on to look at the words in the Stage 15 checklist, many of which are included in 'lūdī fūnebrēs'.

First language note (relative clauses)

The language note emphasises the clause rather than the relative pronoun. The aim is to enable the pupils to identify relative clauses, translate them appropriately and identify the noun to which each clause refers. Discussion of the pronoun is postponed until the pupils have met more examples in their reading; it is referred to in the context of gender agreement in Stage 18 and discussed more fully in the Unit IIB Language Information pamphlet.

After the language note has been read, the class might look back at the model sentences and at one or more of the earlier stories in the stage, picking out examples of relative clauses and the nouns to which they refer. Identification of clause boundaries can usefully be practised by requiring two pupils to read each sentence; one reads the relative clause, the other the main.

Manipulation exercises and suggestions for further practice

Exercise 1   Type: completion
              Missing item: verb
              Criterion of choice: morphology
              Linguistic feature being practised: present tense of *sum*,
                 introduced in Stages 4,5 and 10

Exercise 2   Type: completion
              Missing item: noun
              Criterion of choice: morphology
              Linguistic feature being practised: accusative and dative
                 singular, introduced in Stages 2 and 9; and accusative
                 and dative plural, introduced in Stages 8 and 9

This stage would be a suitable time to begin consolidation work based on
the 'About the language' section of the Unit IIA Language Information
pamphlet. See pp.35–6 below for commentary.

Second language note (nōnne?)

nōnne was first introduced in Stage 13 and should now be reasonably
familiar. Pupils will probably find it convenient to think primarily of
'surely' and 'surely . . . not' as translations of *nōnne* and *num*, but idiomatic
and varied alternatives (e.g. 'You don't mean to tell me that Bregans is
working ?') should be encouraged. It is often helpful to have such
sentences (and their translations) read aloud with appropriate intonation.

The background material

The evidence of Cogidubnus' life and career is extremely scanty and
depends on only two ancient references:
Tacitus, *Agricola* 14

> *quaedam civitates Cogidumno regi donatae (is ad nostram usque memoriam*
> *fidissimus mansit), vetere ac iam pridem recepta populi Romani consuetudine, ut*
> *haberet instrumenta servitutis et reges.*

Certain territories were given to King Cogidubnus (he remained most
loyal right down to our own times) according to an old and long-
accepted tradition of the Roman people – using even kings as
instruments of slavery.

The dedicatory inscription (*R.I.B.* 91) from a temple to Neptune and Minerva at Chichester; see pupil's text p.57. The drawing there is based on the following reconstruction.

[ ] = missing part of stone; ( ) = expansion of abbreviation.

[N]EPTVNO ET MINERVAE
   TEMPLVM
[PR]O SALVTE DO[MVS] DIVINAE
[EX] AVCTORITAT[E TI(BERI)] CLAVD(I)
[CO]GIDVBNI R[EG(IS) MA]GNI BRIT(ANNORUM)
[COLLE]GIVM FABROR(VM) ET QVI IN EO
[SVN]T D(E) S(VO) D(EDERVNT) DONANTE AREAM
. . .]ENTE PVDENTINI FIL(IO)

(Note: In the drawing of the inscription in the pupil's text, the form COLEGIVM reproduces the presumed original. A letter E with a slightly extended foot is a common epigraphical ligature for LE, so the word can be read as the usual COLLEGIVM.)

The reading of the inscription adopted here is based on 'King Cogidubnus in Chichester: Another Reading of *RIB* 91', J.E. Bogaers, *Britannia* X, 1979, 243–54. Bogaers rejects the traditional reading of line 5 – [CO]GIDVBNI R(EGIS) LEGAT[I] AVG(VSTI) IN BRIT(ANNIA) – which suggests that Cogidubnus was an imperial *lēgātus,* an unparalleled rank for a non-Roman.

Both references, the second in particular, have been the subject of scholarly debate and in the absence of further evidence are likely to remain so.

Cogidubnus' career is therefore highly controversial (see e.g. Cunliffe, *Excavations at Fishbourne,* vol. I.13–14; 'The career of Tiberius Claudius Cogidubnus', A.A. Barrett, *Britannia* X, 1979, 227–42). It is possible that he was educated at Rome and/or that he had control of the Atrebatic kingdom between the flight of the king, Verica, and the arrival of Claudius. The kingship may have been a reward for services rendered to Claudius in the invasion. It had been important to Claudius that the invasion should succeed, as he had been extremely anxious to gain some personal military prestige. Cogidubnus' tribe was given a Roman name (Regnenses), and the dedication of the Chichester temple to Minerva, goddess of culture, may say something about the progress of Romanisation; the dedication to Neptune is explained by the town's position close to the sea.

We have adopted Cunliffe's view that Cogidubnus was the owner of Fishbourne, although it must be stressed that there is no direct evidence. Certainly this most unusual building could be explained as a mark of imperial favour towards a loyal client-king. Pupils may find the chronological sequence of the background section difficult. It refers mainly to the time of the height of Cogidubnus' power, when the palace was built and lived in, but the first and penultimate paragraphs look back to the earliest years of the conquest. If further information is needed on the early (military occupation) period, see Cunliffe, *Fishbourne*, ch.3. The evidence for the granary, worth mentioning briefly (granaries will be important in Unit IIIA), is closely set vertical timbers, providing a raised floor to keep corn dry and well ventilated (for a reconstruction see C.S.C.P. *The Romans discover Britain* p.63).

It is worth discussing with pupils the evidence for Cogidubnus' life as an elementary introduction to the historian's use of source material. Explain to pupils that a historian, like a detective, has to draw deductions from evidence; that often it is impossible to draw *certain* deductions, only *probable* or *possible* ones; and that the historian's task is to decide which conclusions are more likely and which less. It is important to let the pupils voice their own views and think for themselves (basing their speculation on the evidence), before intervening or starting to direct the discussion. Pupils may be surprised to find that there is no one 'right' answer.

Suggestions for discussion

1 Ways in which Cogidubnus may have helped Claudius or Vespasian in A.D. 43 and other methods by which he may have demonstrated his support for Rome.

2 What the term 'client-king' meant, and how his relationship with Rome would have been viewed by the Romans, his own subjects and himself.

3 Ways by which Britain was 'Romanised'.

4 How far the pupils would have supported Cogidubnus, had they been ordinary Regnenses.

Suggestions for further work

The background topics of Stage 15 (King Cogidubnus) and Stage 16 (The palace at Fishbourne) are closely linked and may if desired be taken together. For some suggested activities, see pp.33–4.

Words and phrases checklist

See under 'lūdī fūnebrēs', p.24 above.

STAGE 16: IN AULĀ

Synopsis

Reading passages } { King Cogidubnus   } (continued from
Background material } { the palace at Fishbourne } Stage 15)

Main language features   pluperfect
                          further infinitive usages

Model sentences

Cogidubnus gives Quintus a conducted tour of his palace and holds a
banquet for his guests. It is worth emphasising the magnificence of the
palace and its Italian style – comparisons could be drawn with the
Pompeian houses of Unit I. The entertainment is also Romanised – and
rather bizarre. The dancing-girl who appears from the egg, and the
juggling dwarfs, are not untypical of entertainment at the dinner parties
of rich Romans (for other examples see e.g. Petronius, *Cena Trimalchionis*
53 etc., Pliny, *Letters* IX.17).

The new language feature, the pluperfect tense, is used only in relative
clauses in this stage; the context will often guide pupils to the correct
meaning. A translation 'had' should be insisted on for the time being.
Detailed discussion of the morphology should be postponed until the
language note has been read. The relative clauses now include examples
introduced by *quōs* and *quās*.

The following words are new (but their meanings should be clear from the
pictures): *fōns, marmoreus, effundēbat, ōvum, saltātrīx, pīlās, iactābant.*

Belimicus ultor

The discomfiture of Belimicus in Stage 15 has an unexpected sequel,
which is described in this and the following story. Outraged personal
pride drives him to look for means of vengeance, but his evil plans go
astray and virtue finally prevails. The events in the stories depend closely
on the emotions of the characters. Class discussion might well be directed
towards this aspect and questions asked on the following lines:

How did Belimicus react to his defeat in the boat-race?
Which Latin words and phrases describe his mood?
What was the attitude of other people towards Belimicus in his
    misfortune?

Whose mockery would be particularly annoying to Belimicus? Why?
Did the other Cantici feel the same?
Is this true to life? Is this how the defeated behave?
What do you imagine Belimicus' thoughts and feelings might have been
    while he was training the bear?
Finally, ask pupils what they expect Belimicus will do to gain his revenge.

The presence of the bear in this stage is not merely to provide story
interest; it points also to the Roman fondness for using animals for
display, particularly, though not exclusively, in the amphitheatre.
Cogidubnus is imagined as owning a collection of wild animals, cared for
by a special slave who would bring them out on occasions such as this to
show to guests. The capture of these animals in the provinces of the
empire and their transport to Rome was big business. Bears and wolves
were imported from Britain and Germany, lions from North Africa,
elephants from East and Central Africa and crocodiles from the Nile
valley. Most of them were destined for the *vēnātiōnēs* in the amphitheatre,
while some went to zoological collections kept by wealthy men in private
parks. There are some points of comparison here with modern interest in
zoos, safari parks, animal films and expeditions. For the Roman interest
in animals see Balsdon, pp.302ff., Jennison, and Toynbee. For lively, if
gruesome, end-of-term reading, see 'Thrasyleon' in C.S.C.P. *The Roman
World* Unit I Book 4 *The Witches of Thessaly* (a story from Apuleius about a
private animal park).

Language work based on this story could involve picking out and
retranslating the relative clauses and identifying the nouns to which they
refer, as in Stage 15.

Consolidation using the Language Information pamphlet should also
continue through Stage 16. This story contains several examples of the
irregular verbs *sum, volō* and *possum* – see Language Information
pamphlet, p.10.

rēx spectāculum dat

This story is the climax of the Belimicus episode. The first reading should
be done at one sitting if possible; it might be translated rapidly by the
class working together with occasional help from the teacher, or the first
part could be dealt with by simple comprehension questions. In the
following lesson, details of motive and plot could be discussed and
language points studied. The following questions might be asked:
Why are Salvius and Quintus near the king (lines 1–2)?
Why do the Romans, not the Britons, show interest in wine?
Why does Belimicus make no reply to Dumnorix' taunts?
How do we know that the bear is well-known before this story starts?

Why is Belimicus *furēns* (line 31)?

Why do you think Salvius stands motionless?

The story could then be read again as a play, with parts for narrator(s), Dumnorix, Salvius and Belimicus. Special attention should be paid to tone of voice in Belimicus' '*īnsolēns*' speech and Dumnorix' reply. The class might be asked to contribute appropriate sound effects.

Language work could concentrate first on relative clauses again. Encourage idiomatic alternatives to the literal translation, for example:

sed ursam, quae saltat, vidēre volō. (lines 13–14)

But I want to see the dancing bear.

ego, quem tū dērīdēs, ursam tractāre audeō. (lines 21–2)

You laugh at me, but I have the nerve to handle the bear.

This may be a convenient point at which to repeat some examples of word order from the Unit I Language Information pamphlet pp.13–14, as a purely aural exercise, in which the pupils do not have a sentence in front of them but listen to it being read by the teacher (see Unit I Handbook, p.25). This may provide some helpful practice of the accusative + verb sentence pattern, in readiness for some more complex examples of this pattern in the next story (see below under 'Quīntus dē sē').

Pupils sometimes raise the question 'Who is the more important, Salvius or Cogidubnus?' They could be encouraged to attempt an answer themselves, based on what they may have read in the stories. The distinction between Cogidubnus' titular power and Salvius' real superiority may begin to emerge; a final answer to the question should be reserved until pupils reach the later developments in Unit IIIA.

Quīntus dē sē

This short linking passage prepares for Alexandria, the theme of Unit IIB. In answer to the king's questions, Quintus begins to recount the story of his life after the death of his parents at Pompeii. The passage should be read quickly, perhaps using the printed questions instead of translating. Alternatively pupils might tackle the questions on their own or in groups, before the passage is gone through in class.

Further questions could be asked about characters and events (N.B. the answers are not all contained in this story):

Why do you think the king is now so friendly to Quintus?

What was the name of Quintus' mother?

In Quintus' third sentence, what is implied about the fate of Grumio and Melissa?

What do you think was the name of the freed slave? (Clues in the paragraph, plus a recollection of Stage 12, should suggest Clemens.)

How had Clemens shown himself *tam fortis et tam fidēlis* (line 7)?
 (See Stage 12 'ad vīllam' and 'fīnis'.)
In what direction did Quintus and his *lībertus* sail when they were going
 ad Graeciam (line 12)? And *ad Aegyptum* (line 16)?
There are two examples in this story of relative clauses introduced into
the accusative + verb sentence pattern:
 line 7 *servum, quī . . . fuerat, līberāvī.*
 line 9 *omnēs vīllās, quās . . . possēderat, vēndidī.*
The lack of an expressed subject may cause difficulty; if so, the teacher
could usefully make up further examples of this pattern.

First language note (pluperfect tense)

After reading the note and translating the examples, it may be helpful to
go back to the model sentences, pick out examples of the pluperfect and
retranslate them. Invite pupils to comment on paragraph 4 of the
language note; the similarity in form between the perfect and pluperfect
tenses might be further emphasised by asking pupils to say what the
perfect would be, given a sentence containing the pluperfect, and vice
versa.

Manipulation exercises and suggestions for further practice

Exercise 1 Type: completion
        Missing item: noun
        Criterion of choice: sense and morphology
        Linguistic feature being practised: nominative and dative
            plural, introduced in Stages 5 and 9
Pupils may need reminding of the spelling of 'Britons'.

Exercise 2 Type: translation
        Linguistic feature being practised: imperfect and perfect
The Durotriges were the tribe occupying the area around Dorchester.
Pupils could be asked why they think Cogidubnus helped the Romans.
Whether Vespasian had the palace built for Cogidubnus is controversial
(see p.26). Besides the services to Vespasian mentioned here, Cogidubnus
might conceivably have helped to keep the legions in Britain loyal to
Vespasian in his bid for the principate in 69.
 After the exercise has been translated, it could be used for practising
the verb in a substitution exercise, with variation of both person and
tense, e.g.
 What did *Durotrigēs fortiter pugnāvērunt* mean?
 Now what would *fortiter pugnābam* mean?

The second exercise contains two examples of a new sentence pattern, dative + accusative + verb: *Rōmānīs frūmentum comparāvī. Rōmānīs explōrātōrēs dedī* (line 5). The pattern has previously been met only in subordinate clauses (like *mihi auxilium . . . dedistī* in line 16 of the same exercise) and further practice with additional examples may be advisable if the pattern causes difficulty. An example (*vigilibus rem nārrāvit*) is included in Attainment Test 4 below. The pattern recurs in Unit IIB and is practised in the IIB Language Information pamphlet, p.19.

Second language note (further infinitive usages)

Examples from the stories could usefully be picked out for practice. 'rēx spectāculum dat' is the best quarry.

The background material

The site of the palace is close to the sea; in Roman times it was even closer to the shore-line and there was a quay only a few yards from the south wall of the palace. The earliest buildings on the site were military. They belong to the invasion period of A.D. 43, and may have been connected with Vespasian's attack on the Isle of Wight or his drive against the Durotriges to the west. By about A.D. 75 civilian buildings, constructed of timber and masonry, appear, among them a remarkable set of baths with at least seven heated rooms, larger than the contemporary public baths at Silchester. The evidence suggests the presence by this date of a civil settlement of some size, having trading connexions with Italy.

In A.D. 75 or thereabouts, work began on the palace itself. When finished, it consisted of four wings containing some sixty to seventy rooms, round a colonnaded courtyard. The total complex, which occupied an area of just over 2.25 hectares (5½ acres), has been described as 'a piece of Italy planted in Britain'. Two examples may be given of the expert skill lavished upon it:

The builders' working-area
Excavation uncovered a builders' working-area spread over six rooms. The whole area was blanketed in white sand from 2.5cm to 30cm thick, containing waste pieces of Purbeck marble, red and buff coloured mudstone from the Mediterranean, grey shale from the Weald and a small quantity of marble imported from central France and Italy. The work that went into the preparation of this decorative stone may be surmised from the calculation that in this working-area there were 3.7 cubic metres (130 cubic feet) of waste stone. Examination of the waste suggests that the different operations involved – chipping, chiselling, grinding and sawing – were each performed in a separate part of the area.

At the point where the sawing appears to have been done, the largest deposits of sand were found. This required some explanation and an experiment was carried out. It was found that a piece of marble could be cut effectively by means of a six-strand twisted copper wire in a hacksaw frame with the aid of sand and water; and the kind of cut made was exactly the same as that left by the Roman masons. This method of stone-cutting is still used in parts of Italy today.

The products of the workshop included patterned stone pieces of pavements, panels and beading for wall veneers, small decorative pieces possibly for inlaying on furniture and various household utensils such as pestles and mortars. Nearby were found traces of a service road used for bringing building material to the site, and there were also some remains of timber buildings where the workmen may have lived. One can imagine the organisation required to get such an operation going and to sustain it.

The garden of the Great Court
Here again the work of experts is apparent. They removed over 5,350 cubic metres (7,000 cubic yards) of surface clay and gravel to expose the underlying clay bed. This was then resurfaced with topsoil. It is worth reminding pupils of the immensity of the labour involved in moving earth – compare, for example, the huge machines used in modern motorway construction. Shrubs and bushes were then planted in a specially prepared mixture of loam and crushed chalk to counteract the acidity of the soil. Roses too were planted in specially dug beds. The whole garden had a formal arrangement reminiscent of the garden of Pliny's villa in Tuscany. There is an unmistakable impression of Italy and Italian skill.

The most detailed description of the excavations will be found in Cunliffe, *Excavations at Fishbourne*. An account for the general reader is given in Cunliffe, *Fishbourne*.

Suggestions for discussion

1 Discuss the variety of craftsmen probably employed in the building and decoration of the palace at Fishbourne. What materials and tools did they use? Compare these with the materials, tools and sources of power employed on a modern building. (See Neuburger, and Strong and Brown.)

2 With the aid of appropriate pictorial material, such as frames from Filmstrips 1 and 2, discuss with pupils the evidence for describing the palace as 'a piece of Italy planted in Britain'. Pupils, working in groups, could produce pamphlets or posters to illustrate, by plans, pictures and notes, the similarities in architecture, interior decoration, gardens, baths, etc., between the palace at Fishbourne and Italian villas. (See Filmstrip 1 frames 2–5, 7–15; Unit I slides 1–26; Filmstrip 2 frames 7–13; Unit II

slides 2–19. See also pictures in pupil's text, pp.65,69,71 and 75. For examples of other provincial work for comparison see Filmstrip 2 frames 5–6, 14–15; Unit II slide 18; Unit III slides 34–5.)

Suggestions for further work

1   Ask pupils to write an imaginative account *either* of a visit by Cogidubnus to the palace while under construction (he may be showing it to a visiting chieftain, e.g. Dumnorix), *or* of masons at work cutting stone and marble in the masons' yard. Encourage pupils to be as detailed as possible about the skills and methods employed on the site.

2   Show slides or filmstrip frames or other pictures of the mosaics at Fishbourne, including the second-century Dolphin Mosaic and read the poem 'Dolphin Mosaic' by Ian Serraillier (in Jones, Jones and Hayhoe) about its loss and rediscovery. (See filmstrip 10–12; slides 10–14 and 16–17. These include a detail from the Dolphin Mosaic. See also the picture in the pupil's text, p.63.)

3   The museum and site at Fishbourne are open to the public. For special party rates apply to the Curator, Palace Museum, Fishbourne, Sussex. (A visit to Bignor Roman Villa can often be fitted in on the same day.)

The Language Information pamphlet

This pamphlet consists of two sections, 'About the language' and 'Words and phrases'.

The 'Words and phrases' section is a reference vocabulary for the whole of Unit IIA. Its format is explained in notes on p.14 of the pamphlet. It is suggested that the teacher go through these notes with the class, in particular sections 2,3 and 4 which explain and practise the new layout of the verb; additional examples can be made up on similar lines.

The 'About the language' section is intended for reference by the pupils, and for consolidation. For notes on its use see Unit I Handbook, p.82. This section is retrospective in character and would not be very suitable for introducing new points.

Work on the exercises in this section might begin when the pupils reach Stage 15 and thereafter be kept going *pari passu* with the reading of Stages 15 and 16, with some exercises perhaps being postponed until Stage 16 has been completed. They are generally more difficult than those in the stages and are designed to be used *after* the pupils have had a fairly lengthy reading experience of the linguistic feature being practised.

The following comments are concerned with individual sub-sections:

Nouns (pp.4–5). When pupils are working on the transformation exercises in paragraphs 2 and 3 of this sub-section, it remains important to emphasise the link between a word's morphology and its function in the sentence; the complete Latin sentence should therefore normally be read out and translated before and after each singular-to-plural or plural-to-singular transformation, though this rule will occasionally have to be relaxed in the interests of pace. Pupils working on these exercises will sometimes need a little guidance in manipulation of 3rd declension nouns; they should be shown how to consult both the table of nouns in paragraph 1 and (where necessary) the entry for the relevant noun in the 'Words and phrases' section. The exercise in paragraph 4 provides a convenient opportunity to assess the pupils' grasp of the dative, followed if necessary by further practice; they are about to meet the genitive in Stage 17, and it is desirable that at this point their handling of the dative should be accurate and confident.

Verbs (pp.8–9). The forms of the present, imperfect and perfect tenses are given, also the infinitive. The pluperfect tense does not occur in the reading material until Stage 16, where it is described in a language note for pupils to refer to while reading that stage. All four tenses will be given in the Language Information pamphlet for Unit IIB; in Unit IIA, the main emphasis should fall on the present, imperfect and perfect.

The present tense of all four conjugations is given in full. In the imperfect and perfect tenses, the forms of the first conjugation are printed in full, and other conjugations are shown in the forms of the 1st and 2nd person singular only, to emphasise the extent to which all four conjugations follow the same principle in forming these tenses.

Irregular verbs (pp.10–11). The present tense of *sum, possum, volō* and *nōlō* is shown, together with the imperfect of *sum* and *possum*. If pupils ask about the imperfect tenses of *volō* and *nōlō*, explain that these tenses are entirely regular; this might be demonstrated to the pupils by giving them a few examples for translation, preferably with an infinitive attached, e.g. *labōrāre nōlēbant*, etc.

Longer sentences (pp.12–13). Study of paragraphs 6 and 7 of this sub-section, which provide an opportunity for examining the way in which relative clauses normally begin and end, might be preceded by the revision of some familiar examples of relative clauses, e.g. from the first Stage 15 language note (p.54), and the question 'How can you tell where a relative clause begins and ends?' The pupils will very likely reply 'By the commas', in which case ask them if it would still be possible to tell, even without the commas; on looking again at the examples, they will probably suggest that the clause begins with *quī* or a similar word and that the verb comes at the end of the clause. Confirm that this is the usual (though not invariable) pattern. The pupils might also be asked to consider how sentences containing relative clauses should be read aloud. At this point, paragraph 7 in the present sub-section can be tackled, in which the relative clauses are printed without commas. Pupils could be asked to indicate the relative clause by reading it out, or (perhaps better) by reading the *whole sentence* aloud, slightly emphasising the pause before and after the relative clause.

Linguistic synopsis of Unit IIA

This synopsis follows the same plan and is designed for the same purposes as the Unit I linguistic synopsis described on page 84 of the Unit I Teacher's Handbook. When reading a stage with a class, teachers are strongly advised to concentrate on the features dealt with in that stage's language note(s), rather than attempting discussion and analysis of every feature listed here. LI=Language Information pamphlet.

Stage	Linguistic feature	Place of language note etc.
13	infinitive + *possum, volō, nōlō*	13
	present tense of *possum* and *volō*	13,LI
	-que	13
	questions with *nōnne?*	15
	perfect passive participle	21
	clauses with *quamquam* and *simulac*	LI
	nominative singular of 2nd declension neuter nouns	
	omission of verb in second of two clauses	
	clauses with *ubi* (= 'when')	
	sēcum	
	apposition (nominative)	
	nominative predicative adjective	
14	attributive adjective (met from Stage 3): agreement of case and number	14
	imperfect of *possum*	14,LI
	infinitive + *decōrum, difficile*, etc.	16
	vocative in *-ī*	19
	nōlī (one example)	19
	imperative plural (one example)	19
	present participle	20
	ipse	
	apposition (accusative)	
	accusative predicative adjective	

Stage	Linguistic feature	*Place of language note etc.*
15	relative clauses with nominative singular and plural and accusative singular of *quī*	15,LI
	questions with *nōnne?* (met from Stage 13)	15
	infinitive + *dēbeō*	16
	omission of verb in first of two clauses (one example)	
16	pluperfect (in relative clause)	16
	infinitive + *decōrum, difficile*, etc. (met from Stage 14), *dēbeō* (met from Stage 15) and *audeō*	16
	relative clauses with accusative plural of *quī*	
	relative clauses in sentences with subject omitted	
	DATIVE+ACCUSATIVE+VERB word order (two examples)	

The following terms are used in Unit IIA. Numerals indicate the stage in which each term is introduced.

infinitive	13
adjective	14
agree(ment)	14
number	14
relative clause	15
pluperfect	16
pronoun	LI

Appendix A: Attainment test

For notes on the purpose of the attainment tests, and suggestions for their use, see Unit I Handbook, p.88. The words and phrases in heavy type are either new to pupils or have occurred infrequently in the reading material.

Test 4

To be given at the end of Stage 16.

somnium mīrābile

Sextus et Titus erant amīcī. ad urbem **iter faciēbant**. postquam ad urbem pervēnērunt, Sextus ad tabernam contendit. Titus tamen apud frātrem manēbat. post cēnam Titus, quod fessus erat, mox obdormīvit. subitō Sextus in **somniō** appāruit et clāmāvit,

'amīce! caupō mē necāre vult. necesse est tibi mē **adiuvāre**.'   5

Titus statim surrēxit, quod **commōtus** erat, et sibi dīxit,

'num caupō amīcum meum necāre vult? minimē! somnium erat.'

Titus iterum obdormīvit. Sextus iterum in somniō appāruit et clāmāvit,

'ēheu! mortuus sum. caupō **scelestus** mē necāvit. postquam mē necāvit, in plaustrō mē **cēlāvit**. tū eum pūnīre dēbēs.'   10

Titus ē lectō perterritus surrēxit et **vigilēs** petīvit. vigilibus rem nārrāvit. tum cum duōbus vigilibus ad tabernam contendit. caupōnem rogāvit,

'ubi est Sextus, amīcus meus, quī in hāc tabernā manēbat?'

'**errōrem** facis', caupō eī respondit. '**nēmō** est in tabernā.'   15

Titus, ubi plaustrum in viā cōnspexit, clāmāvit,

'ecce! amīcus meus, quem tū necāvistī, in hōc plaustrō **cēlātus** est.'

vigilēs, postquam plaustrum īnspexērunt, Sextum invēnērunt mortuum. caupōnem attonitum **comprehendērunt**, et eum ad iūdicem dūxērunt.   20

On *vigilibus rem nārrāvit* (lines 11–12) see note on Stage 16 exercise 2, p.32 above.

Appendix B: Words and phrases in Unit IIA checklists

The numeral indicates the stage in which the word or phrase appears in a checklist.

advenīre (13)
aedificāre (16)
aedificium (13)
aeger (13)
agmen (15)
alius (15)
alter (13)
antīquus (14)
apud (14)
aqua (15)
argenteus (14)
attonitus (14)
aula (14)
auxilium (16)

bonus (16)

cantāre (13)
cēterī (13)
claudere (15)
commodus (15)
coniūrātiō (13)
cōnsentīre (16)
cōnsilium (16)
cotīdiē (14)
custōs (13)

dēbēre (15)
dēcidere (15)
decōrus (14)
deinde (16)
dēlectāre (16)
dēlēre (14)
dērīdēre (16)
deus (14)
dīcere (13)

dictāre (14)
difficilis (14)
dīligenter (14)
dīmittere (16)
domina (14)
dōnum (14)

effigiēs (15)
effugere (16)
equus (15)
etiam (15)
excitāre (13)

faber (16)
familiāris (14)
fessus (13)
fidēlis (14)
flōs (16)
fossa (15)
frāctus (15)
frūmentum (16)

geminī (13)

haurīre (13)
honōrāre (15)
horreum (13)

impedīre (15)
imperātor (16)
inter (16)
interficere (13)
ipse (14)
iste (14)
ita (16)
ita vērō (13)

lavāre (14)

lectus (15)
lentē (15)
lītus (15)

marītus (14)
melior (16)
miser (15)

nauta (15)
nāvigāre (16)
necesse (14)
nōbilis (14)
nōlle (13)
nōnne? (16)
novus (13)
nūllus (13)
num? (14)
numerāre (13)

ōrdō (13)

parātus (16)
perīre (16)
plaustrum (15)
pōnere (16)
posse (13)
postrīdiē (16)
praeesse (15)
pretiōsus (14)
prīnceps (15)
prior (15)
pūnīre (16)

quam (= 'how') (14)
quamquam (14)
-que (14)
quī (15)

redīre (15)

retinēre (13)

rēx (14)

ruere (13)

sacerdōs (15)

saltāre (16)

saxum (15)

sē (13)

sella (14)

simulac (16)

suāviter (13)

summus (16)

superesse (16)

tenēre (15)

tollere (16)

trahere (13)

ubi (= 'when') (14)

unda (15)

velle (13)

vertere (16)

victor (15)

vincere (15)

vulnerāre (13)

Appendix C: Summary of changes from the first edition of the course

Most of the changes listed in Unit I Handbook, p.94, apply also to Unit IIA. Other changes to Unit IIA include the following:

1 Stages 13–16 have been bound together in book format.

2 New **vocabulary** has been reduced by about 35 words.

3 The use of the perfect passive participle in conjunction with forms of *esse* has been restricted to those occasions where it can be treated simply as an adjective; sentences where the required sense of (for example) *interfectus est* is 'he was killed' have been excluded.

4 Words in the glossaries of the **reading passages** are given both in the form in which they occur in the passage and in their 'basic' form (e.g. nominative of noun, infinitive of verb) and glossed accordingly.

5 The new **'About the language'** notes include two notes in Stage 14 dealing with agreement of adjectives.

6 The **background material** for Stages 13 and 14 has been extensively rewritten; a new reading has been adopted for the Cogidubnus inscription quoted in Stage 15.

7 In the **'Words and phrases checklists'** and the 'Words and phrases' section of the **Language Information pamphlet**, verbs are shown in the form of the 1st person singular of their present tense, followed by their present infinitive and the 1st person singular of their perfect tense.

Bibliography

Books

The following is a select bibliography on Roman Britain and other themes relevant to Unit IIA. Many of the recommended books are out-of-print (O.P.) but they are included in case teachers already possess them or can obtain second-hand copies. Books marked * are suitable for pupils.

Andrews, I. *Boudicca's Revolt* (Introduction to History of Mankind series: C.U.P. 1972)

Apicius. *The Roman Cookery Book*, trs. B. Flower and E. Rosenbaum (Harrap 1974)

Balsdon, J.P.V.D. *Life and Leisure in Ancient Rome* (Bodley Head 1969)

Birley, A.R. *Life in Roman Britain* (Batsford rev. edn 1976)

Burn, A.R. (ed.) *The Romans in Britain: an anthology of inscriptions* (Blackwell 1967 O.P.; U.S.A. University of South Carolina Press 1969)

Cambridge School Classics Project. *The Romans Discover Britain* and *Teacher's Handbook* (C.U.P. 1981)
   The Roman World Units I and II (C.U.P. 1978–9)

Clayton, P.A. (ed.) *A Companion to Roman Britain* (Phaidon 1980)

Collingwood, R.G. and Richmond, I.A. *The Archaeology of Roman Britain* (Methuen rev. edn 1969)

Cottrell, L. *The Great Invasion* (Evans 1958 O.P.)
   Seeing Roman Britain (Pan rev. edn 1967 O.P.)

Cunliffe, B. *Excavations at Fishbourne 1961–69* (Society of Antiquaries 1971)
   Fishbourne: a Roman Palace and its Garden (Thames & Hudson 1971 O.P.)
   The Iron Age Communities in Britain (Routledge 1978)
   The Regni (Peoples of Roman Britain series: Duckworth 1973)

Doncaster, I. and Bullard, I. *The Roman Occupation of Britain* (Evidence in Pictures series: Longman 1961 O.P.)

Dudley, D.R. and Webster, G. *The Rebellion of Boudicca* (Routledge 1962)

Durant, G. *Britain, Rome's Most Northerly Province* (Bell 1969 O.P.)

Fishbourne Roman Palace. *Educational Wallet* (contains posters and booklets: available from the site)
   Young Visitor's Guide (Macmillan with the Sussex Archaeological Trust 1973)

Fox, Lady A. and Sorrell, A. *Roman Britain* (Lutterworth Press 1961)

Frere, S.S. *Britannia: a History of Roman Britain* (Routledge rev. edn 1978)

Green, M. *Roman Technology and Crafts* (Aspects of Roman Life series: Longman 1979)

Jennison, G. *Animals for Show and Pleasure in Ancient Rome* (Manchester University Press 1937 O.P.)

Jones, D. and P. *The Villas of Roman Britain* (Jackdaw series: Cape 1973 O.P.)

Jones, E.H., Jones, B. and Hayhoe, M. (eds) *Roman Britain* (Themes series, paperback: Routledge 1972) Recommended. An anthology of sources in translation, poetry and extracts from historical novels.

Liversidge, J. *Britain in the Roman Empire* (Routledge 1968)
   Furniture in Roman Britain (Academy Editions 1973 O.P.)
   Roman Britain (Then and There series: Longman 1968)

London Association of Classical Teachers. Lactor No.4: *Some inscriptions of Roman Britain* (L.A.C.T. 1971)
   Lactor No.11: *Literary Sources for Roman Britain* (L.A.C.T. 1977)

Longman. *Roman Britain History Project Kit* (Longman 1971 O.P.)

Margary, I.D. *Roman Roads in Britain* (Baker 3rd edn 1973)

Neuburger, A. *The Technical Arts and Sciences of the Ancients*, tr. H.L. Brose (Methuen Library Reprints 1969)

Ordnance Survey. *Map of Roman Britain* (H.M.S.O. 1979)

Percival, J. *The Roman Villa* (Batsford 1976)

Pliny. *Letters: a selection*, tr. C. Greig (C.U.P. 1978)

Priestley, H.E. *Britain under the Romans* (Warne 1967 O.P.)

Richmond, Sir I.A. *Roman Britain* (Pelican new issue 1970; U.S.A. Barnes and Noble)

Rivet, A.L.F. *The Roman Villa in Britain* (Studies in Ancient History and Archaeology: Routledge 1969)
   Town and Country in Roman Britain (Hutchinson 1966; U.S.A. Hillary)

Rule, M. *Fishbourne Roman Palace Guide* (Sussex Archaeological Society 1977)
   Floor Mosaics in Roman Britain (Macmillan 1974 O.P.)

Salway, P. *Roman Britain* (Oxford History of England, Vol.IA: O.U.P. 1981)

Sellmann, R.R.S. *Roman Britain* (Methuen 3rd edn 1964 O.P.)

Sorrell, A. *Roman Towns in Britain* (Batsford 1976)

Strong, D. and Brown, D. (eds) *Roman Crafts* (Duckworth 1976)

Sunday Times *Roman Britain Wallchart* (Times Books 1978 O.P.)

Susini, G. *The Roman Stonecutter* (Blackwell 1973 O.P.)

Tingay, G. *From Caesar to the Saxons* (Longman 1969)

Toynbee, J.M.C. *Animals in Roman Life and Art* (Aspects of Greek and Roman Life series: Thames & Hudson 1973 O.P.)

Wacher, J. *Roman Britain* (Dent 1978; Pbk 1980)

Webster, G. *Boudica: British Revolt against Rome A.D.60* (Batsford 1978)
   The Roman Invasion of Britain (Batsford 1980)

Rome Against Caratacus: the Roman Campaigns in Britain A.D.48–58 (Batsford 1981)

Roman Britain: a map produced for The Observer (distributed by George Philip 1978 O.P.)

Webster, G. and Dudley, D.R. *The Roman Conquest of Britain A.D.43–57* (British Battles series: Batsford 1966 O.P.; Pan 1973 O.P.)

White, K.D. *Country Life in Classical Times* (Elek 1977)

Wilson, R.J.A. **Guide to the Roman Remains in Britain* (Constable 2nd edn 1980)

Historical novels for pupils

Duggan, A. *The Little Emperors* (Faber 1951 O.P.)

Kipling, R. *Puck of Pook's Hill* (Macmillan 1951; Piccolo 1975)

Marris, R. *The Cornerstone* (Long Ago series: Heinemann 1976) A story about the son of a Fishbourne mosaicist.

Plowman, S. *To Spare the Conquered* (Methuen 1960 O.P.) Set at the time of the conquest of Britain and Boudica's revolt.

Ray, M. *The Eastern Beacon* (Faber 1965 O.P.) The adventures of a young Greek girl and Roman boy who are shipwrecked on the Scilly Isles in the 3rd century A.D.

Spring Tide (Faber paperback 1979) Two boys encounter Christianity for the first time.

Seton, A. *The Mistletoe and the Sword* (Brockhampton 1956 O.P.) Set at the time of Boudica's revolt.

Sutcliff, R. *The Eagle of the Ninth* (O.U.P. 1954; Puffin 1977) A young Roman officer tries to recover the lost eagle of the vanished Ninth Legion. Perhaps the best of its kind.

The Silver Branch (O.U.P. 1957; Puffin 1980) Sequel to the above, set 170 years later.

The Lantern Bearers (O.U.P. Pbk 1972; Puffin 1981) A Roman soldier remains after the withdrawal from Britain and helps to fight the invading Saxons.

Outcast (O.U.P. 1955; Pbk 1979) A young British tribesman is sold into slavery.

Treece, H. *Legions of the Eagle* (Bodley Head 1954; Puffin 1965) The story of a boy living during the invasion of A.D.43.

War Dog (Brockhampton 1962 O.P.) A story about Bran, the huge war dog of Caractacus' charioteer.

The Queen's Brooch (Hamilton 1966 O.P.) The life of a young Roman who encounters Boudica.

Wheeler, M. *The Farthermost Fort* (Dent 1969 O.P.) This story centres on the final withdrawal from Britain.

Bibliography

Source material for the Roman world generally
Lewis, N. and Reinhold, M. *Roman Civilisation: a Sourcebook. I The Republic; II The Empire* (Harper Torchbooks: Harper and Row 1966)

Reference
C.I.L. – *Corpus Inscriptionum Latinarum* (Berlin, 1863–)
Dessau, H. *Inscriptiones Latinae Selectae* (Berlin, 1892–1916)
R.I.B. – Collingwood, R.G. and Wright, R.P., *The Roman Inscriptions of Britain* (O.U.P. 1965)

Slides and filmstrips

This list contains general surveys of Roman Britain and topics of particular relevance to Unit IIA. Further Roman Britain titles appear in the Unit IIIA Handbook, particularly those exclusively concerned with the army. The list is only a selection and makes no claim to be exhaustive. Slides on many towns and sites are available from the local museum; these slides are not listed here, though many are included in the sets produced by Pictorial Colour Slides. The Department of the Environment publishes slides of the more important monuments in its care, showing air views in many cases, and reconstruction drawings, many of which are by Alan Sorrell. These are available at the site or a catalogue may be obtained from the address in the list of suppliers.

Addresses of suppliers are given at the end of this list.

Chapman, Hugh. *The Museum of London: Roman exhibits*. 9 slides, colour, notes. Reconstructions of kitchen and two dining-rooms, carpenter's and blacksmith's tools, cutler's stall, Mithras head and relief of Mithras and bull with zodiac around, strainer from Wallbrook Mithraeum. (Woodmansterne OL 10; Slide Centre W 289)

Davies, D. Garret (adviser). *Roman Britain: the towns*. Filmstrip, single or double-frame, colour, 46 frames, brief notes, cassette optional. Takes Verulamium as its starting point. Attempts to add interest and clarity by the use of plentiful models and reconstructions, and even actors. (Hugh Baddeley, HB 113)

Green, A.C. *et al. The Roman City; The Roman Villa; Roman Roads; Roman Forts and Walls* (People of Other Days series). This is a series of fairly short (about 20 frames) single-frame colour filmstrips, using entirely artists' reconstructions (lively and accurate) to examine aspects of Roman Britain in some depth. Notes. Cassettes optional. (Visual Publications PD 1–4)

Lishman, E.P. *Roman Britain*. Filmstrip, double-frame, colour, 50 frames, notes. A recent strip (1980) of good quality with a strong military bias.

Frames are sometimes horizontal and sometimes vertical, so may be
better cut up and used as slides. (Focal Point, Half-century series)

Peckett, C.W.E. *Roman Britain*. Filmstrip, double-frame, 43 frames, full
notes and suggestions for pupils' work, cassette optional. Part of Visual
Publications' Adventure of Man series, this strip begins with a brief
account of the conquest, and passes on to the army, roads, towns,
housing, Bath, Cirencester, a mosaicist's workshop, Dolaucothi gold mine
and religion. Uses reconstructions as well as photographs. (Visual
Publications MAN 11/3)

Pictorial Colour Slides. This firm publishes many slides of archaeological
sites and objects from Roman Britain. They will not supply single slides
but issue sets including the following:

Prehistoric: *Iron Age ornaments and metalwork* (set 7); *Iron Age coins, pottery and
combs* (set 8)

Roman: *Field monuments* – 15 slides of miscellaneous town and fort sites
(set 10); *Hadrian's Wall* – 20 slides (set 11); *Models and reconstructions,*
including much military material, e.g. ballista – 25 slides (set 12);
Roman gods and emperors – 25 slides (set 13); *Roman sculpture* – 10 slides
(set 14); *Inscriptions, coins and tile stamp,* including military tombstones –
20 slides (set 15); *Mosaic pavements* – 12 slides (set 16); *Bronze and silver
tableware* – 10 slides (set 17); *Roman glass vessels* – 15 slides (set 18);
Roman pottery – 40 slides (set 19); *Domestic objects* – 15 slides (set 20);
Personal ornaments – 10 slides (set 21); *Burial and other objects* – 12 slides
(set 22)

Slide Centre. *Life in Roman Britain*. 16 slides, colour, brief notes. Vigorous
and highly coloured reconstructions more appropriate for younger pupils.
Map of Britain would be more useful with names. (Slide Centre 262)

Smith, D.J. (adviser). *Roman Britain: Fortifications*. Filmstrip, single or
double-frame, colour, 45 frames, brief notes, cassette optional. Includes
Hadrian's Wall and Saxon Shore forts. Models as well as photographs of
sites (Hugh Baddeley, HB 115)

Taylor, D. *Ancient Rome Parts I and II*. Filmstrips, double-frame, colour, 33
frames in each + titles, cassette, notes. These Radiovision strips have
specific aims and succeed by not trying to do too much, by evocative
photography and by imaginative commentary (narration by the she-wolf
of Rome, a centurion, etc.). Intended as an introduction to Roman studies
primarily for children of 10 to 12.

Strip One includes the foundation of Rome; ruins in the city and
around the empire; temples, roads, aqueducts, gates; the ethics of empire;
celebration of empire in art; Roman Britain (Dover lighthouse,
Porchester, Bath, Caerleon, Hadrian's Wall).

Bibliography

Strip Two includes more on Roman Britain (Corbridge, Lullingstone, pots, glass, silver, hypocausts, London, ships and trade); Ostia; Pompeii; model of ancient Rome.
(BBC; Slide Centre BBC 39,40)

White, H.A.B. and H.R.B. Roman Britain series. A series of excellent filmstrips devoted to individual sites, including Bignor, Londinium, Verulamium, Corinium, Chedworth, Silchester and Roman Leicester, as well as Fishbourne and Bath which are listed separately below and in the Unit IIIA Handbook respectively. (H.A.B. White)

Material appropriate to particular stages

Stage 13
Forder, T. *Early Man in Britain: 7 Iron Age.* 18 slides, colour, notes. A rather fragmented set of plans, diagrams and photos, including a good one of a reconstructed Iron Age house at Butser Hill. (Slide Centre Rickett Sl379)

Todd, K. *Greek and Roman Farming.* Filmstrip, double-frame, colour, 44 frames (including 20 on Roman farming), full notes and suggestions for pupils' work. Commentary available on cassette. The Roman section is primarily about farming in Italy. (Visual Publications MAN 12/1)

Stages 15 and 16
White, H.A.B. and H.R.B. *Fishbourne Roman Palace.* Filmstrip, double-frame, colour, 36 frames, notes. Includes an air view of the site, plans, views of the garden, floors, a number of museum exhibits including painted wall-plaster, and the Cogidubnus inscription. (H.A.B.White)

Addresses of suppliers

Hugh Baddeley Productions, 64 Moffats Lane, Brookmans Park, Hatfield, Herts. AL9 7RP
Department of the Environment, Clerk of Stationery, Department of the Environment, Victoria Road, South Ruislip, London
Focal Point, 251 Copnor Road, Portsmouth, Hants.
Longman Group Ltd., Longman House, Burnt Mill, Harlow, Essex CM20 2JE.
Pictorial Colour Slides, 242 Langley Way, West Wickham, Kent.
The Slide Centre Ltd., 143 Chatham Road, SW11 6SR.
Visual Publications, The Green, Northleach, Cheltenham GL54 3EX
H.A.B. White, 79 Teddington Park Road, Teddington, Middlesex.
Woodmansterne Colourslides, Holywell Industrial Estate, Watford WD1 8RD

Unit IIB

Introduction

Unit IIB (Stages 17–20) is set in Alexandria, in the form of a flashback which covers the period between Quintus' escape from Pompeii in A.D. 79 and his arrival in Britain in A.D. 82; a further link with Unit I is provided by Clemens, the former slave of Caecilius. Quintus acts as narrator. The Alexandrian setting provides a contrast both with the small-town atmosphere of Pompeii and with the rural Romano-British background of Unit IIA; in some respects, the picture of life in a great city foreshadows that of Rome itself, to which the pupils will be introduced in Unit IIIB.

The main linguistic advance in Unit IIB is the introduction of the genitive case into the basic sentence patterns, while the patterns themselves increase in complexity and become more variable in their word order. But the chief emphasis, as in Unit IIA, is less on the introduction of new linguistic features than on the consolidation of features already met. Thus, discussion of agreement of the adjective is extended to cover gender; such pronouns as *hic* and (in oblique cases) *is*, which have been met many times by pupils in their reading, are now explicitly discussed. It is important that by the end of Stage 20 pupils should have a secure grasp of the linguistic points discussed and consolidated in Units IIA and IIB, so that they can give their full attention to the major linguistic advances that lie ahead. In particular, they need to be confident and accurate in dealing with the four tenses (present, imperfect, perfect and pluperfect) and the four main cases (nominative, accusative, genitive and dative) described and/or practised in this section of the course.

Of the various manipulation exercises that practise morphology, those in the stages concentrate especially on the verb, while those in the Language Information pamphlet tend to focus on the noun (thus reversing the emphasis in the corresponding sections of Unit IIA); the suggestions for oral work in the stage commentaries below are mainly concerned with morphology of the noun and adjective.

The advice in the Unit I Handbook (p.9) is repeated here, that it is normally desirable for schools with a four-year course to finish Stage 20 by the end of the first year, and for schools with a three-year course to have made inroads into Unit IIIA by that point; also that it is better to omit occasional stories here and there during the year than to make more drastic cuts, or omit an entire stage, at the year's end. Some of the following passages in Unit IIB might be read quickly or omitted (with a résumé supplied if necessary by the teacher) by those whose time allowance is short:

Stage 17   'ad templum'
Stage 18   'Clēmēns tabernārius'
Stage 19   'pompa' or 'nāvis sacra'
Stage 20   'Petrō' or 'fortūna crūdēlis'

For suitable visual material dealing with Alexandria, see Bibliography, p.92. For the benefit of those teachers who are using the Unit II slides which accompanied the first edition of the course, reference to particular slides is given in this Handbook. Some of the original slides have been incorporated into the pupil's text as photographs. There is no material specifically on Alexandria in Cambridge Classical Filmstrip 2, though frame 28 (Isis and Serapis) could be useful. There are also some frames on Alexandria in the Additional Filmstrip (Cambridge Classical Filmstrip 4).

The cassette

The first of the two cassettes accompanying the course includes the following material from Unit IIB:

Stage 17   'ad templum'
Stage 18   'prō tabernā Clēmentis'
Stage 19   'pompa'
Stage 20   'astrologus victor'

Stage commentaries

Books are normally referred to by the name of their author. For details of title, publisher, etc., see Bibliography, pp. 90–91.

A list of the linguistic features introduced and discussed in each stage is given in the 'Linguistic Synopsis of Unit IIB' on pp. 81–2.

STAGE 17: ALEXANDRĪA

Synopsis

Reading passages } the city of Alexandria
Background material }

Language notes   genitive singular and plural
position of *enim*, *tamen* and *igitur*

Model sentences

Quintus continues the account which he began to give Cogidubnus in 'Quīntus dē sē', Stage 16. Pupils may need to be reminded of this. The model sentences focus on some of the more striking features of Alexandria and introduce Barbillus, a wealthy Roman businessman, who will play a leading part in Unit IIB. The pictures contain much detail and pupils may find it helpful to discuss each picture for a few moments before tackling the text beneath. Why, for instance, is Quintus making a sacrifice (p.3)? Why are he and Clemens both unshaven? What does the magnificent atrium of Barbillus' house suggest about him?

The genitive case is introduced in this stage, with one example in each group of model sentences. For the moment its occurrence is limited to prepositional phrases, such as *in portū Alexandrīae*. The context of the new case has also been carefully designed. Thus, in paragraph 1, the phrase *in portū Alexandrīae* is preceded by sentences in which the nouns *portus* and *Alexandrīa* occur. Experience has shown that, given this framework, the new case is likely to be grasped with little or no difficulty by most pupils.

The new words and phrases are glossed.

tumultus

Quintus goes to live as a guest in the house of Barbillus who is a former business acquaintance of Caecilius. With Barbillus' help, he has

52

established Clemens, now a freedman, in the glass trade which flourishes near the harbour. In the present stage the scenes of Alexandrian life are observed through the eyes of Quintus; the experiences of Clemens are recounted in Stage 18. 'tumultus' is a story of racial tension and conflict, and it illustrates certain common characteristics of such tensions: that they are easily aroused, erupt quickly into violence, are directed at the nearest available target and frequently involve the innocent. Pupils, especially those living in urban areas, are likely to notice the topicality of this theme without prompting. If the class is mature enough, it may be useful to explore with them some of the causes – social, economic, cultural – of bad relationships between ethnic groups, and ways and means of easing or containing the problem. Why were the Egyptians envious and hostile towards the Greek population in Alexandria? Why were the Jews in conflict from time to time with non-Jews? (This question could lead to the subject of the Jewish revolt in A.D.66–70 and its final tragedy, at Masada, in A.D.73. The story is told in Unit IIIB.)

The multi-racial nature of Alexandrian society often put the Roman governor in difficulties, for he could do little to modify the basic clash of interests between the social groups and generally was obliged to rely heavily on police and military enforcement of public order. For centuries the Greeks had occupied the highest positions of power, wealth and influence; they formed a close-knit community that knew how to protect its advantages. Opposed to them were many other groups, Syrians, Egyptians, Jews, all competing for a share of prosperity in what was to them the rather alien environment of a Greek city. Though we should not overestimate the civil violence, there is no doubt that Alexandria was a turbulent city. Vigorous and competitive trade was its daily occupation; riot was perhaps a daily hazard.

For literary evidence of racial attitudes in the ancient world see Juvenal, *Satires* III and XV and the relevant epigrams of Martial (e.g. XI.96).

The sentence *nam in casā . . . vituperābat* (lines 31–2) may cause difficulty, since the point of the first half of the sentence only becomes clear when the second half has been read. Question 5 in the pupil's text, and reference back to lines 20–1, may help.

Some suggested questions

Why do you think the old man was making a speech?
What might he have said?
Why was Quintus worried (line 22)?
Why did he whisper rather than speak aloud (line 28)?
Why did Diogenes feel it necessary to keep a supply of clubs in his house?

ad templum

Barbillus and Quintus encounter Plancus, an erudite and tenacious pest who, like the similar character in Horace, *Satires* I.9, shows himself impervious to polite discouragement. The god Serapis, who was worshipped in conjunction with Isis, was the guardian deity of Alexandria and connected especially with the harvest and with healing. A fuller discussion of religious activity is given in Stage 19 but it should be noticed here that:

1 The large statue of the god was placed in the *cella*, or inner sanctuary, of the temple. Only priests and members of the brotherhood of Isis would enter this part of the temple; ordinary people would see the statue only when it was brought out for a religious festival.
2 The performance of public ritual, e.g. the sacrifice, took place outside the temple, not inside. Contrast the position of the altar of a modern Christian church with that of the altar of a classical temple.
3 The public were spectators, not participants in the religious act. For more information see Marlowe 59–61.

The picture on p.9 shows Serapis crowned with a basket or corn measure, indicating his connection with crops and fertility. The head was found in the Mithras temple, at the Walbrook, London, showing mutual toleration of cults.

The passage is suitable for drama work. Emphasise the character of Plancus and the barely concealed exasperation of Barbillus.

vīdistis (line 25) or *vultis* (line 32) may be a good starting point for a substitution exercise to help consolidate the verb (see Unit I Handbook p.24 for suggestions). Pupils might be asked, for example, for the meaning of *vīdit* and *vīdērunt*, or of *sacrificium vidēre volumus* and *Plancus garrīre vult* and similar short phrases and sentences.

Some suggested questions

Why was Barbillus reluctant to reply (line 10)?
Why did Plancus eventually *have* to keep quiet?
Would you have found Plancus a nuisance? If so, why?

First language note (genitive singular and plural)

This brings together examples of the genitive case, and points to common contrasts between the form of the nominative and genitive. The further examples should provide a useful check on pupils' grasp of the sense of the new case. The teacher might next ask pupils to pick out other examples of the genitive already met in the two previous stories. Encourage variety in translation. Thus,

in portū Alexandrīae
may produce: in the harbour of Alexandria
          or: in the harbour at Alexandria.

per viās urbis
may be translated by: through the city streets
                 or: through the streets of the city.

in vīllā Barbillī
should lead to the English apostrophe formation: in Barbillus' house.

mercātor Arabs

Of the many traders who regularly converged on Alexandria from the east (see map, pupil's text p.16), some came by sea to the Red Sea ports and then down the Nile, while others used the overland routes through the desert. Arab traders brought gems, perfumes, silk and other precious goods for the rich markets of the Roman world; they also brought strange tales of desert travel. The essence of such tales is grotesque incident, sudden wealth and miraculous escape from disaster. The source of this passage is 'The Second Voyage of Sinbad' in the *Arabian Nights*.

Some suggested questions

   How could you set up an ambush in the desert?
   What do you think the merchant expected the monster to do when it flew at him?
   Why in fact did the monster fly at the merchant?
   What caused his belt to shine?
   How would you have tried to escape from the nest?
   Would you have taken anything with you?
   Which parts of the story do you find hardest to believe?

As a stimulus to discussion invite a pupil to draw the monstrous bird on the blackboard; then ask other volunteers to add anything omitted by the first pupil. Pupils often search the text with minute care looking for details in the description.

   These questions can be followed by contributions from the class of other travellers' tales involving encounters with strange creatures, abnormal working of nature, extravagant incident, and dramatic reversals of fortune. The teacher might provide an example of a strange creature from Caesar, *De Bello Gallico* VI.27, a species of elk without joints in its legs.

   Language work in this stage should include some revision of the relative clause and the pluperfect tense. To do this, pupils can be asked to pick out examples of relative clauses and their antecedents in 'tumultus' or 'ad templum' (six examples are contained in each) and to identify the pluperfect tenses in 'mercātor Arabs'. In any discussion, it is important always to relate abstract terms such as 'relative clause' and 'antecedent' to concrete examples.

The pluperfect tense, hitherto restricted to relative clauses, will appear from this point in main clauses as well.

mercātōrem fortūna servāvit (p.12, line 38) is the first example of a sentence with the pattern accusative + nominative + verb. More examples will follow in Stages 18 and 19, together with the pattern accusative + verb + nominative. These patterns are practised in the Language Information pamphlet. Comment to the class is not necessary at this point.

Manipulation exercises

Exercise 1   Type: completion
Missing item: verb
Criterion of choice: morphology
Linguistic feature being practised: 1st and 2nd persons
   singular and plural of imperfect and perfect tenses,
   introduced in Stage 12

Exercise 2   Type: completion
Missing item: verb
Criterion of choice: sense and morphology
Linguistic feature being practised: 1st, 2nd and 3rd persons
   singular of present tense of *volō* and *possum*, introduced in
   Stage 13

This exercise could be followed by further practice of the present tense of *volō* and *possum*. Use the pronoun markers *ego, tū* etc. at first; then withdraw them. It is better to include an infinitive with each example, e.g. *currere possum, festīnāre volumus.*

Second language note (position of enim, tamen and igitur)

This draws attention to the position of these connectives in the sentence and invites comparison with the position of their English equivalents. One or two further examples could be picked out from the stories.

The background material

The aim is to help pupils to think of Alexandria as a city whose size, culture and economic importance made it unique in the eastern Mediterranean at this time. Focus discussion on these aspects:

1 Its size, layout and population. Perhaps a million people lived in an architect-designed conurbation spread over many square kilometres. It had been built up from nothing but a fishing village to be a showpiece of Alexander's empire. In the hands of his Greek successors, the Ptolemies, the city's natural advantages of large, safe anchorages on major trade routes were consolidated; the arts and scholarship flourished under royal patronage; Alexandria became a very prosperous, international commercial centre.
2 The style and method of its government. The administration was autocratic, with power concentrated in the hands of the Greek community. A highly developed bureaucracy controlled the life of the Egyptian peasants and villagers, whose work was prescribed to them in detail and whose freedom was severely restricted.
3 The city as a manufacturing centre. For instance, it was famous for its glassware.
4 The city as the focal point of a very wide trade network. See the map in the pupil's text, p.16.
5 The tensions that existed between the racial groups living in the city. For evidence of anti-semitism see Lewis and Reinhold, II.413. Older pupils could attempt comparisons with some of our contemporary problems such as prejudice against ethnic minorities, and the increased resort to violence as a form of protest.
6 The contrasts between life in Alexandria, Pompeii and Roman Britain. Levels of material comfort, cultural richness, personal freedom and the general pace of life would have varied sharply between these places as well as between social groups. Younger pupils might be invited to consider where they would have preferred to live and to debate their reasons.

Visual evidence of Alexandria in the classical period is scanty. Virtually nothing remains to be seen and this deficiency makes it difficult for pupils to imagine the scale and splendour of the ancient city. Something, however, of the atmosphere may be recaptured by reading extracts from Evans (now unfortunately out of print but very useful if you can find a copy). Also helpful are group projects which require pupils to explore and prepare accounts of different aspects of city life. Some suggestions are given below.

The map on p.16 shows the extent of the empire at the time of the stories, and indicates the main movements of goods both within and from outside the empire. Alexandria's importance as a trade centre for both raw materials and manufactured goods is clear. Silk came from China, pepper from India and ivory from central Africa. It is also interesting to note that Rome imported far more than she exported: this she paid for with her revenue from the provinces.

The coin illustrated on p.17 underlines the importance of shipping in Alexandria and of Isis as protectress of shipping.

Words and phrases checklist

The genitive is now included in the checklists. Its meaning can be emphasised by asking the class for a translation not only of *hasta, latrō* etc. but also of *hastae, latrōnis* etc.

Suggestions for further work

1 The idea of a city. Begin by obtaining data about any large modern city: its population, area, main industries, public amenities, university, local government and the diversity of its population. Ask pupils to prepare a short guidebook on the basis of this information. Then ask them to use such sources as Lewis and Reinhold, Marlowe, Forster and the information in the pupil's text to prepare a similar guide to Alexandria. Compare the two and discuss the changes that have followed from the effects of modern technology. (If this project is tackled, it is worth looking into the possibility of liaison with other departments, such as geography or civic studies.)

2 Consider Alexandria as a port. Ask pupils to list major imports and exports, indicating where possible the origin of the goods; draw a large plan of the Great Harbour; study the Pharos lighthouse and compare its mode of operation with a modern lighthouse; explore the evidence for the trade routes commonly used by land and sea, the kind of shipping and the length of some of the voyages made (see the map, pupil's text p.16; Lewis and Reinhold II.198–208; *Penguin Atlas of Ancient History* 84–5; Hodge, Ch.V). Also invite pupils to think about ways in which a large port, e.g. London, Liverpool, Cardiff, New York, Boston, Montreal, may differ from a large town that is not on a waterway: mixture of nationalities, influx of new ideas and customs, a large migrant population, the presence of trades and industries that relate primarily to ships and sea-faring.

3 Invite pupils to write an imaginary newspaper account, including an editorial, a feature article and eye-witness reports, of a riot either between Jews and Greeks or between Greeks and Egyptians. ('tumultus' could be used as a basis.) They should comment on the causes of the riot, the consequent damage and the problem of law and order in the city. Some Greek names might be Apollonius, Dionysus, Hermaiscus; Jewish names, Philo, Josephus, Theophilus, Markos; Egyptian names, Phaseis, Zoilus and Haryotis. A variation on this activity is to ask pupils to write two contrasting newspaper reports, dealing with the same incident but written for newspapers having different editorial sympathies. Encourage

pupils to be subtle in the way they reveal these sympathies.

4   Set a competition for the best story on the lines of 'mercātor Arabs'. Attention should be paid to the setting in which the tale is told. The possibilities are many, e.g. a silk trader talking to Barbillus, a ship's captain talking to a wholesaler who has just purchased a consignment of Arabian perfume, etc. The aim is to tell a fantastic story in as convincing a manner as possible. Pupils might appreciate a reading of the second and fifth voyages of 'Sinbad the Sailor' before written work is attempted.

STAGE 18: EUTYCHUS ET CLĒMĒNS

Synopsis

Reading passages	} { economic and commercial life in Egypt
Background material	} { glassmaking

Language notes   agreement of adjective (gender)
                             verbs with dative (continued from Stage 11)

Model sentences

The model sentences describe the assault, referred to in the first story, on Barbillus' old freedman. Discussion could focus on the characters in the picture and the reasons for their behaviour and expressions.
Linguistically the sentences illustrate agreement of gender but discussion of this point should be postponed until the first language note has been dealt with. There is no new vocabulary.

taberna

This story explains how Clemens comes to own the shop referred to in Stage 17 'tumultus': he is established in the business by Quintus, who buys the shop for him from Barbillus. The latter warns Quintus of the local mafia who operate a protection racket and have been responsible for the murder of the previous tenant, his old freedman. Quintus, however, asserts that Clemens is well able to look after himself.

During this and the following story pupils could be given revision practice in picking out nouns of the nominative and accusative singular and plural. The teacher's questions might vary between, e.g. in 'in officīnā Eutychī' 'What case is *servōs* in line 18?' and 'Find a nominative in line 12 and say whether it is singular or plural'.

Some suggested questions

What would be the advantages of putting all the glassware shops together in the same street? What would be the disadvantages?

Do you agree with the description of Clemens as *vir fortis*? If so, why? (Pupils will probably remember Clemens' actions in Unit I, Stage 12.)

in officīnā Eutychī

This story brings out the contrasting characters of Clemens and Eutychus and offers an insight into the workings of a glass factory.

valvās ēvulsās vīdit, tabernam dīreptam (lines 5–6): accept the simple translation 'he saw the torn-off doors, the ransacked shop' but encourage better alternatives such as 'he saw the doors which had been torn off' and 'he saw that the doors had been torn off and the shop looted'.

officīnam Eutychī (line 18): this phrase pattern, with the genitive depending on a nominative or accusative noun, is new but occurs only once in this stage. It is practised extensively in Stage 19 and no comment therefore is needed at this point.

Some suggested questions

Why does Clemens call the slave '*Atlās*' in line 15?

Why does Clemens refer to himself as *lībertō* rather than *mihi* in line 17?

Why does Eutychus display his thirty slaves to Clemens?

Pupils could be asked to compare the price of the protection (10 *aureī*) with the price of the shop (100 *aureī*). They might also be invited to say why such rackets are generally regarded as wrong. A possible question might be 'From what are the purchasers buying protection?'

Clēmēns tabernārius

The religious element of Alexandrian life, touched on in Stage 17 'ad templum', reappears here, when Clemens joins the brotherhood of the goddess Isis and is initiated into the mysteries and the communal life of the cult. The members of the brotherhood meet regularly to celebrate the sacred meal, study the scriptures, sing hymns and pray. The analogies with the liturgy and the sacraments of the early Christian Church are striking and are discussed under Stage 19 on page 70 below. Some pupils may ask for more information about Isis and, although the main discussion should be postponed to Stage 19, when the subject is explored more fully, a preliminary comment along the following lines could be helpful: Isis was one of Egypt's most important goddesses, one of a closely related group of three deities – Isis, Osiris and Horus. She was

worshipped for her power to give new life in the form of crops in the
spring or after the flooding of the Nile. She also offered hope of life after
death to her followers.

   In addition to the questions in the pupil's text that follow this story,
pupils could be reminded of the context of the story by being asked on *ut
dīxī*, line 7, who the speaker is and to whom he is speaking. They might
also be invited to comment on Clemens' policy of taking care not to
overcharge, which is mentioned in the last sentence of the first paragraph.
Do they think he would have made more profit by pushing his prices up?
When discussing the picture, ask whether Clemens looks *cōmis*. Consider
also the reasons for the presence of the cat. Cats were kept by Egyptians
as pets and to protect the Alexandrian granaries from rats and mice. They
were also venerated as sacred animals. Why is it particularly appropriate
for there to be a cat in Clemens' shop?

First language note (adjective agreement: gender)

The note begins by referring to the rule of agreement between nouns and
their adjectives in respect of case and number (see language note in Stage
14, p.26). Take pupils through the note and work through the examples.
Pupils should then look again at the model sentences of this stage,
identifying the adjectives and the nouns they agree with. (Under the
teacher's guidance, the class could work out the Latin for 'the slave-girls
were terrified'. This identification exercise can be extended to the stories.
Phrase the questions sometimes in linguistic terms ('Which noun does
īrātus describe?') and sometimes in content terms ('Who was angry,
Clemens or the shopkeeper?'). Further practice of noun + adjective
agreement could be devised for subsequent lessons on the lines of the
exercise contained in paragraph 4 on page 7 in the Language Information
pamphlet.

   From now on the nominative masculine singular form of adjectives is
included in the story glossaries.

prō tabernā Clēmentis

Clemens hears the news that his shop has been looted by Eutychus and
his thugs. Far from being dismayed, Clemens shows the calm faith of one
who believes the gods protect the just and punish the guilty; he stands up
to the thugs and is duly rewarded by help from the sacred cat. Take this
story at a brisk pace, as pupils will be keen to find out what happens next.
The story is particularly suitable for drama work (see Unit I Handbook,
p.21).

   ubi ā templō, in quō cēnāverat, domum redībat, amīcum cōnspexit accurrentem
(lines 2–3) is a new sentence pattern containing two subordinate clauses,

one of which (*in quō cēnāverat*) 'nests' within the other (*ubi ā templō . . . domum redībat*). The task for the pupil is to handle the interruption of one statement to accommodate another, and to recognise the clause boundaries. To help with this, commas have been used, for the time being, to mark the boundaries.

If, when translating *tabernam tuam dīripiunt Eutychus et operae,* line 4, pupils produce a passive rendering, the teacher should not dismiss it as wholly wrong but encourage a rephrasing beginning with Eutychus.

As further consolidation of ability to recognise the dative case in context, it may be helpful to ask pupils to pick out examples, stating whether singular or plural, from stories in this stage. This will prepare the ground for the language note on p.36.

Sentences containing clauses with *postquam, quod, simulac* etc. taken from the Language Information pamphlets of Unit I (p.15) and Unit IIA (pp.12–13) could also be revised at this time in the form of an aural exercise as suggested in the Unit I Handbook (top of p.82).

Some suggested questions

Why do you think Clemens is not impressed by Eutychus and his thugs? Was it because his piety or religious faith protected him from fear? Or had he learned to stand up for himself during his former life as a slave? How did Clemens behave before he became a freedman?

What do you think of the thugs' reactions to the cat? Credible? Incredible? (Pupils' views often differ surprisingly at this point.)

Manipulation exercises and further practice

Exercise 1 Type: completion
Missing item: noun + adjective phrase
Criterion of choice: morphology
Linguistic feature being practised: nominative singular and plural, introduced in Stages 1 and 5

Exercise 2 Type: completion
Missing item: verb
Criterion of choice: morphology
Linguistic feature being practised: 3rd person singular and plural of pluperfect tense, introduced in Stage 16

In sentence 2 pupils will probably treat *dīrepta* as an adjective and say 'was ransacked'. Occasionally a pupil may ask 'Would it be clearer to say "had been ransacked"?' This suggestion should be approved, as better in the context, but teachers are recommended *not* to anticipate the discussion of the indicative passive which is presented in Unit IIIB.

Exercise 3   Type: completion
              Missing item: verb
              Criterion of choice: sense and morphology
              Linguistic feature being practised: 1st and 2nd persons
                  singular of perfect tense, introduced in Stage 12

Different types of perfect tense formation are included in this exercise: the
perfect stem in -s-, the strong perfect stem, and the perfect stem in -v-.
The teacher should observe whether some types cause more difficulty
than others and, if necessary, make up further examples, keeping the
vocabulary simple and familiar and the sentences short.

Revision of the noun could continue. Using the paradigm on pp.4–5 of the
Language Information pamphlet, pupils could be asked to translate the
underlined words in such sentences as 'I gave a reward to the girl', 'he
killed the lions', etc. Exclude the genitive case from this kind of exercise
until the class has met more examples of it.

Second language note (obstō, resistō, etc. with dative)

A number of verbs of this kind have now been met. When the note has
been studied, more examples selected from previous stories can be put on
the board or the teacher may wish to make up simple sentences
containing these verbs.

The background material

The first section develops the topic of glassmaking, already touched on in
the stories; the second section deals with certain aspects of Egyptian
economic life, in particular the exploitation of the peasant farmers and the
high degree of centralisation, bureaucracy and corruption. For further
information about the economic life of Egypt, see Lewis and Reinhold
II.198–208, 363–4, 397–400; and Fraser I.132ff; for glassmaking, see
Dodsworth, Harden and the section by J. Price in Strong and Brown 111ff.
    The picture on p.38, of a glass-blower at Pye Unicam, Cambridge,
shows the continuity of the technique described in the background
material.

Words and phrases checklist

From now on, 1st and 2nd declension adjectives are shown in these lists in
the form of the masculine, feminine and neuter nominative singular; 3rd
declension adjectives are usually shown in their masculine form only.
Check that pupils are clear about this, for instance by asking them 'What
would be the Latin word for "dangerous" if it described a woman?' 'What

is the neuter form of the word for "long"?' A few examples of this sort will help to ensure that pupils grasp the significance of the layout.

Suggestions for further work

1   Read with the class extracts from the *Acts of the Apostles*, e.g. 19.23–41; 21.27–40; 22.1–30, and discuss them as instances of civil disturbance in the provinces.

2   Let pupils imagine they are the Greek whose list of bribes is quoted in the stage and invite them to write a story about how and why they gave one of the bribes. Remind them to set the stories in a suitable atmosphere of corruption and tyranny by local officials.

3   If you have or can borrow a copy of Lindsay, *Daily Life* (now out of print), give pupils a selection of data from pp.258ff and ask them to construct an account of life on the estate of Lucius Bellenus Gemellus at the time of our story. Epagathus is the supervisor.

4   Pupils could do a piece of artwork on glassware. Pictures of Roman glass can be drawn and coloured (see slides 32–9); coloured postcards and slides are available from many museums; refer to the publications noted above, p.63.

5   An alternative activity for a small group would be to explore the history of glassmaking, including modern technical advances, and to present an illustrated report to the rest of the class. See Dodsworth.

STAGE 19: ĪSIS

Synopsis

Reading passages   ⎫
Background material   ⎬ Isis worship

Language notes   *hic*
                      imperative (including *nōlī, nōlīte*)
                      vocative

Model sentences

These introduce a Greek family: Aristo, his wife Galatea, and his daughter Helena. They watch the spring procession at Alexandria in honour of the goddess Isis. Pupils will be able to understand and discuss the procession better if the relevant parts of the background section are read first.

The genitive case, of which use so far has been restricted to prepositional phrases (with the single exception of *officīnam Eutychī intrāvit*, Stage 18, p.26, lines 18–19), is now introduced in phrases where it depends on a nominative or accusative. The context gives strong clues to the meaning. This new development is not discussed in the language notes of the pupil's text; it is a structural feature that is likely to be grasped better through experience than analysis.

The model sentences also contain several examples of the forms of *hic*, which is discussed in the first language note.

The following word and phrase are new: *castīgat, corōnās rosārum*.

Aristō

This short passage exhibits the new genitive phrases in a very straightforward context. It also adds more detail to the picture of Aristo and his family: Aristo himself is a rather weak man and an unsuccessful writer of Greek tragedies; Galatea, his wife, is a dominating figure, inclined to elbow her way through life; and their daughter Helena is a younger and more frivolous edition of her mother. Neither mother nor daughter shares Aristo's taste in literature; theirs is the popular culture of light music, novels and verse that existed in the Hellenistic world side by side with more serious art.

diēs fēstus

A brisk start may be made by dealing with the first paragraph through comprehension questions alone.

The religious theme of this and the next two stories is discussed in the notes on the background material, pp.69–72 below. When reading these stories with the class try to bring out the sense of holiday, excitement and spectacle. Encourage pupils to visualise the scene. The Alexandrians are thoroughly enjoying themselves and are no doubt dressed suitably for the occasion. Notice too how character emerges from the dialogue. For example, Galatea's shrill peevishness and self-assurance can be heard in *'Helena! nōlī festīnāre! tolle caput!'* (line 14); *'Aristō! nōnne servum māne ēmīsistī?'* (lines 21–2); *'iuvenēs! cēdite! nōlīte nōbīs obstāre!'* (line 35). Aristo's instinct for a quiet life is obvious enough in *'cārissima, melius est nōbīs locum novum quaerere'* (line 30).

In addition to the questions at the end of the story in the text, pupils could be asked to return to the first paragraph and summarise the reasons for the festival. Comparisons could be made with other spring festivals

such as Easter, or the Blessing of the Fishing-nets still conducted in some
English ports, or the Hindu festival of Holi.

Pupils may change the active to passive, producing 'the streets of the
city were now being filled by Alexandrian citizens' for *viās urbis iam
complēbant cīvēs Alexandrīnī* (lines 11–12). The teacher is recommended not
to dismiss this inversion as completely wrong but to guide them to a more
literal version.

This may be a suitable time to begin consolidation work using the
'About the language' section of the IIB Language Information pamphlet.
See pp. 79–80 below for commentary.

pompa

This story may be appreciated at several levels. It may be taken simply as
an amusing incident in the crowd, or as a further study of the characters
of Galatea and Aristo, or as an illustration of the point that people tend to
notice what interests them. Helena's eye is caught by the flowers, the
attention of the young men is drawn towards Helena, while Galatea sees
only the quality of the dress of the statue. It may be helpful to take the
first reading straight and without comment; then, after playing the
cassette recording, the teacher might draw attention to the different
elements by questions such as:

What do you think of Galatea's behaviour towards the two young men?
  Is she fair to Aristo? Give reasons for your answer.
Does Aristo behave towards others in the same way as his wife does?
  Describe the difference between their behaviour.
Why is he a rather unhappy man?
What things in the procession does Helena notice and comment on?
What catches Galatea's eye and what does she say about it?
Do the young men seem to mind not having a good view of the
  procession? Why couldn't they see it?
Which does the story tell you more about, the spectators or the
  procession?

These questions might be followed by asking whether any members of
the class have themselves witnessed a procession or ceremony and
whether they were interested in particular details in the same way as
Galatea and Helena.

The picture on p.52 might be referred to here. From left to right, the
priests and priestesses are carrying a sistrum or rattle (see also the picture
on p.63) and a ladle, a pitcher of sacred water, a scroll, and a water-
vessel. The falcon and lotus headdresses and the cobra are all Egyptian
religious emblems.

The position of *inquit* in the sentence now becomes more idiomatic, e.g.

Helena 'māter' inquit. Pupils may need a little help with this at first.

First language note (hic)

This draws together the forms of *hic* which have already been met. When the note has been read and the examples translated, the teacher can make up further simple sentences for Latin to English translation.
Alternatively, the teacher may use an English sentence, e.g. 'I saw this girl' and ask what the Latin would be for 'this' in the context of the sentence. For either exercise it is important to limit its scope to the forms of *hic* given in the pupil's text and to make the sentences short and simple. It may also be useful to reread the model sentences with particular attention to *hic*. If pupils enquire about a neuter plural form, confirm that it exists but has not yet occurred in the stories.

nāvis sacra

Pupils will find it helpful to have read the background material on pp.62–5 in their text beforehand. They may ask what happened to the ship. As so often with this sort of detail, the evidence is lacking. The view adopted in the story was that the ship was only a ceremonial vessel; she carried no crew and when filled with spices and other offerings she was released from her moorings and allowed to drift out to sea, no one having any thought of seeing her again. An alternative suggestion has been made by Gwyn Griffiths 46–7, who argues that it may have been manned and sent to a destination such as Delos.

Galatea keeps up her flow of admonition and acrimonious complaint. She judges the world from a very self-centred point of view and, as Aristo wrily remarks at the end, fails dismally to understand her own daughter.

If possible, the story should be taken quite briskly so that pupils may appreciate Aristo's final ironic comment '*columba iuvenēs agitat, nōn iuvenēs columbam*'.

See above on 'pompa' for notes on the picture on p.52.

Some suggested questions

What do you think may eventually have happened to the ship?
Is Galatea correct in her view of the effect on Helena of the young men's attention? How do you explain her attitude?
Who understands their daughter better, Aristo or Galatea?

An oral exercise at this point could take the form of asking pupils to pick out examples of the genitive from specified lines of 'nāvis sacra', stating in each case whether the example is singular or plural and adding a

translation. The exercise described above (p.63), based on the paradigm
of the noun in the Language Information pamphlet, could now be
repeated with the genitive case added.

vēnātiō

This is a story of action and danger and a good pace should be
maintained. It prepares the way for the death of Barbillus in Stage 20. At
the beginning try to ensure that pupils understand the initial sequence of
events, since they all happen rather quickly. Barbillus has invited
Quintus and Aristo to a hunt. On the day itself he first sends out Phormio
with slaves and two kids (which will be killed for bait). Then the hunting
party, consisting of Barbillus, Quintus and Aristo, emerges from the
house to set off. At that moment the astrologer rushes up to persuade
them not to go. Stress the atmosphere of foreboding created by the
astrologer's words. Pupils may be able to suggest a St Christopher medal
as a modern equivalent of the amulet. The reference to the Chaldaei in
line 13 points to the main source of astrology in the Hellenistic and
Roman world. The Chaldaei, named after the Chaldaeans whose capital
city was Babylon, were an ancient priesthood; they had developed both
the early scientific study of astronomy and the pseudo-science of
astrology. For more information about the Chaldaei see *Cambridge Ancient
History* XI.642–3.

An interesting account of a hunt on the Nile will be found in Evans
190–5, and more information on hunting generally in Lindsay, *Leisure and
Pleasure* 192–213.

Some suggested questions

Is the astrologer's reason for anxiety convincing? What examples of this
sort of belief about the stars can you suggest from modern life?

Was Barbillus on good terms with his slaves? Use evidence from the
passage to support your answer.

Would you have enjoyed a hunt of this kind?

Second language note (imperative singular and plural, including nōlī, nōlīte)

After working through this note the teacher may find some 'direct
method' techniques helpful for consolidating the point, for instance by
calling for volunteers from the class, directing Latin imperatives at them
and asking them to mime the appropriate action (e.g. *scrībe! sedē! exī! venīte
hūc! dormīte! pugnāte! nōlīte pugnāre!* etc.). Able pupils can sometimes, after

practice, manipulate the Latin well enough to take over from the teacher in giving the orders.

Some pupils, when dealing with *nōlī*, *nōlīte*, may be puzzled by the presence of the infinitive; if so, indicate that *nōlī* literally means 'be unwilling' and invite them to link the infinitive to that version.

Manipulation exercises

Exercise 1   Type: completion
            Missing item: verb
            Criterion of choice: morphology
            Linguistic feature being practised: 3rd person singular and
                plural of perfect tense, introduced in Stages 6 and 7
The exercise should be within the capacity of most pupils and may be set as a written test. It could be followed by work on the 'Verbs' and 'Irregular verbs' sections of the Language Information pamphlet.

Exercise 2   Type: completion
            Missing item: clause
            Criterion of choice: sense, based on the story 'diēs fēstus'
Some pupils may find this exercise difficult. It may be helpful to tackle it first in groups.

Exercise 3   Type: completion
            Incomplete item: noun
            Criterion of choice: morphology
            Linguistic feature being practised: nominative, accusative,
                genitive and dative singular and plural, introduced in
                Stages 1,2,5,8,9 and 17
This exercise is designed to revise all the above cases and to indicate to the teacher whether any of them needs further practice.

Third language note (vocative singular and plural)

The note clarifies the small differences in the spelling of the vocative form of the noun. Invite pupils to study and translate the examples in paragraph 2. The teacher might then direct pupils, by questions, to observe the difference in the vocative of nouns such as *fīlius* and *Salvius* and of those such as *servus*, *Eutychus* and *amīcus*.

The background material

In the Graeco-Roman world of the first century, mystery religions exercised a widespread influence. The cult of Isis, described in Stages 18 and 19, was one of these and is particularly interesting for two reasons. In the first place it was the religion that Alexandria gave to the ancient world. When the Ptolemies imposed on the city a new official state cult, that of Serapis, they associated it with the old Egyptian cult of Osiris and Isis and tried to purge the latter of its more gruesome elements. The cult image of Serapis, created by the Greek sculptor Bryaxis and housed in the Serapaeum designed by Parmeniscus, gave the new god a Greek form (as in the picture of Serapis on p.9 of the pupil's text). Nevertheless, it was the more primitive, life-giving Isis who exerted a stronger hold on people's affections; it was Isis rather than Serapis whose worship spread from Alexandria throughout the Mediterranean. Established in Rome by the first century B.C. she was banished from time to time from the city centre, where only the official Roman deities could properly be honoured. Nevertheless the cult of Isis received official recognition from the Emperor Gaius Caligula and was held in high regard by the Flavian emperors.

Secondly it is interesting to notice parallels between Isis worship and Christianity, discernible, for example, in the cult's concepts of sin, atonement, resurrection, trinity in the godhead (Isis, Osiris and Horus), and also in its modes of worship which included rites similar to Christian baptism and communion, the use of incense, flowers, light, music and choirs and adoration of relics. Such resemblances were not coincidental. Although Christianity inherited some of these liturgical and theological features from its Judaic background, there was also a tendency for the early Christian Church to assimilate from other contemporary religions ideas and practices that were felt to be harmonious with its own outlook.

The first paragraph of the pupil's text summarises briefly the cult myth. Central to it was the theme of life, death and resurrection. In an older version Osiris, brother and husband of Isis, met sudden death by drowning: a reference to the annual inundation of Egypt by the Nile flood. The later account spoke of the murder of Osiris by his brother Seth (known to the Greeks as Typhon) and the dispersal of the pieces of his body over the world: a reference to the planting of crops and fertilisation of the soil. When Isis, aided by her sister Nephthys, had collected the pieces, she restored them to fertility (not to life in the upper world) and thus Horus was born. Helped by Isis he battled against Seth, the embodiment of evil, and eventually succeeded to the divine throne of his father Osiris. At the centre of the myth is the figure of Isis, the mother goddess giving life to the land and all its plants and creatures (hence the scenes of animals painted on the walls of her temples) and also giving the hope of life after death to those who worshipped her.

A powerful impression of the goddess is given by Apuleius in *Metamorphoses* XI.3–4, where she appears in answer to the fervent prayers of Lucius:

Her long thick hair fell softly in ringlets on her divine neck, and was crowned with an intricate wreath in which were entwined all kinds of flowers. Just above her forehead shone a round disc, like a mirror, or like the bright face of the moon, which indicated to me who she was. Vipers rising from the left and right supported this disc, with ears of corn sprouting beside them. Her multi-coloured robe was made of the finest linen; part was gleaming white, part saffron-yellow, part glowing red. But what caught and held my gaze more than anything else was the deep black glossy mantle. She wore it slung across her body from the right hip to the left shoulder, where it was tied in a knot resembling a shield-boss; but part of it was draped in countless folds flowing gracefully to its lowest edge with tasselled fringes. Its hem was interwoven with twinkling stars and in their midst shone the breathing fire of the half moon. But wherever the sweep of that wonderful mantle stirred, it carried with it a garland intertwined with all kinds of flowers and fruit.

The emblems she carried were of different kinds. In her right hand, she held a bronze rattle; its narrow rim was curved like a sword-belt and passing horizontally through it were several slender rods, which sounded shrilly when she shook the handle three times. A gold dish in the shape of a boat hung from her left hand and along the upper surface of the handle an asp was writhing, with its throat puffed out and its head raised, ready to strike. On the goddess' feet were slippers made from palm-leaves, the symbol of victory.

The *nāvigium Īsidis* described in the pupil's text was celebrated each year at the start of the sailing season after the winter storms; it was performed not only at Alexandria but wherever a temple of Isis was situated near the sea. A lively picture of this colourful event is presented by Apuleius in his *Metamorphoses* XI.9–11 and 16–17, translated by Lewis and Reinhold II.576–7. The passion and resurrection of Osiris was also an annual festival. Juvenal mentions the crowd of devotees uttering cries of grief and running to and fro in the ritual search for Osiris (*Satires* VI.533–4)

Services were held daily at the first and eighth hour. They were conducted by white-robed priests and accompanied by music (pipes, sistra and antiphonal choral singing). Liturgy, sacrifice, the sprinkling of holy water and the revelation of a richly dressed image of Isis, like a southern European madonna, all played a part in these services. Pupils might be invited to identify some of these features of the services by studying the picture on p.62. (They might think that the ibises in the foreground are for sacrifice, but they are there either as part of the Egyptian décor or as a symbol of healing. Sacrifices to Isis consisted of milk, honey or herbs and never involved animal life.)

Sacramental meals and private meditation also figured in the discipline for reaching a state of unity with the godhead. There is a bench in the Isaeum at Pompeii which may have been used for personal meditation.

Nevertheless, despite its appeal to human emotion and widespread popularity at the beginning of the Empire, the cult of Isis was virtually dead by the fourth century A.D. Its eventual failure probably arose from numerous inherent weaknesses. Compared with Christianity, it lacked:

A genuine universality. To become an initiate was an expensive matter.
A historical core to its faith. The sufferings of Osiris were mythical.
Moral principles.
Precise theological teaching. Philosophy stood aloof from it.
Social concern or political involvement.
That toughness and intransigence that marked the relationship of the
    Christian Church with rival faiths and civic authorities. Isis
    worship could and did accommodate many other divinities, Roman
    and Greek, and so lost its distinctive identity.

An indication of the spread of the Egyptian cults is provided by a tablet recording a temple to Serapis in the Yorkshire Museum at York. The temple itself has never been found. The stone bears the words: *deo sancto Serapi templum a solo fecit Claudius Hieronymianus legatus legionis VI victricis –* 'Claudius Hieronymianus, commanding officer of the Sixth Legion Victrix, built up from the ground a temple to the holy god Serapis.'

Suggestions for discussion

1   Which religious festivals are marked by public holidays in Britain today? Do pupils think that merry-making is out of place on a sacred occasion? Why did the Romans not think so?

2   Pupils might describe a religious ceremony that they have seen or shared which had some kind of procession or drama in it.

3   If the composition of the class permits it and pupils are sufficiently mature, invite them to compare the forms and styles of worship, perhaps especially relative to major festivals, among the faiths known to them.

Suggestions for further work

1   After reading the stories in this stage and after some class discussion about Isis, pupils might be asked to write a description of an Isiac service as seen by Clemens at Alexandria.

2   The teacher might read to the class suitable extracts from Apuleius *The Golden Ass* which deal specifically with Isis (Penguin, Ch.17,18).

STAGE 20: MEDICUS

Synopsis

Reading passages
Background material } medicine, pseudo-medicine and science

Language notes   present participle
                 oblique cases of *is*

Model sentences

These continue the story of Barbillus' injury sustained in the last story of
Stage 19. They also introduce present participles, singular and plural, in
the nominative case. Occasional examples have already been met in
previous stages, but it is recommended that detailed discussion of this
feature be postponed until the first language note on pp.74–5 is read.

The following words are new: *lectum* (new meaning), *medicum*.

remedium astrologī

The astrologer who had tried to dissuade Barbillus from hunting on an
unpropitious day now prescribes remedies for his injured shoulder. He
lives with Barbillus as a member of the household. It was by no means
uncommon for a wealthy man to keep a soothsayer on his private staff,
and numerous domestic and business matters would be referred to him
for advice as to whether the time was favourable for a particular course of
action. Now the astrologer proposes a form of medical treatment,
claiming that his cures are potent; and he adopts an attitude of
professional rivalry towards doctors. The practice of medicine at this time
belonged to both the rational and irrational domains, an ambivalence
that is not unfamiliar to the modern world. Barbillus tries to get the best
of both. This passage is on the tape.

See Tacitus, *Annals* VI.20–22 for the piquant method by which the
Emperor Tiberius tested the credentials of the astrologer Thrasyllus, and
for the historian's reflections (ch.22) on the credibility of the idea that the
course of human events is predestined.

The picture on p.71 shows medical instruments made of bronze which
were found at Pompeii. At the top are four different types of forceps; in
the centre, from left to right, are polyp forceps, scissors, possibly a lancet,

a rasp probe, a bone forceps and small forceps; on the right are two scalpels; at the bottom are four types of flat probe. The variety suggests a range of surgical processes, as mentioned in the background material, pp.85–6. For other pictures illustrating medicine, see slides 21–3.

Some suggested questions

What sort of person is Phormio?

Why would Barbillus be more likely to trust the astrologer now than before the hunt? Is he completely in the astrologer's hands at this point?

Is the astrologer a fraud? Or does he believe his own claims? What exactly is it that the astrologer claims to know?

Petrō

Petro, a Greek doctor with an excellent local reputation, is called in and sets about applying the techniques of scientific medicine. His methods contrast sharply with those of the astrologer. He has surgical skill; he knows the importance of hygiene; he appreciates that healing is a natural function. In this story Greek science successfully opposes magic. It is hoped that the details of the operation performed by Petro will not be too strong for the more squeamish pupils. Most seem to be untroubled or even positively to enjoy them. Some may ask about the use of vinegar in this context. It is intended as an antiseptic and would also be of some value in the attempt to stop the bleeding. See Majno 186–8, on wine and vinegar as antiseptics.

Some suggested questions

Was Petro right to be angry with the astrologer?

In what ways was Petro's treatment similar to modern medicine?

Not surprisingly doctors attracted criticism and were the butt of popular jokes then as now. The teacher might like to put these two Martial epigrams on the board and invite pupils to help with the translation. Note that in both cases the doctors have Greek names.

languebam; sed tu comitatus protinus ad me
   venisti centum, Symmache, discipulis.
centum me tetigere manus Aquilone gelatae:
   non habui febrem, Symmache: nunc habeo.

                                                   Martial V.9

nuper erat medicus, nunc est vespillo Diaulus:
   quod vespillo facit, fecerat et medicus.

                                                   Martial I.47

For similar material in translation, see C.S.C.P. *The Roman World* Unit I
Item 62.

First language note (present participles)

When the note has been read and the exercises completed, the class may
be given further practice using the 'Words and phrases' section of the
Language Information pamphlet. Put up on the blackboard some present
participles of unfamiliar verbs and ask pupils to look up the verbs under
the appropriate entry and work out the meaning of the participles. Pupils
could also be asked to pick out participles from the model sentences and
stories and say to whom each refers. The teacher's questions should be
framed sometimes linguistically, e.g. (in 'remedium astrologī', line 7)
'Which noun is described by *lacrimantēs*?' etc., and sometimes in terms of
meaning, e.g. 'Who were weeping?' etc.

fortūna crūdēlis

While nursing Barbillus, Quintus learns about his past life. The
happiness of the early years of his marriage has been broken by a family
quarrel which had a tragic ending. When consulted about the prudence of
a proposed family visit to Athens the astrologer had given advice that led
to sharp disagreement between Barbillus and his son Rufus. The
adolescent Rufus presents an oversimplified argument to justify doing
what he wants to do. Pupils who are themselves adolescent may identify
strongly with his point of view. It may be helpful to encourage them to
explore their views a little further: do they think there were other
considerations Rufus should have thought about? Why do they think
Plotina gave way? What may have been Barbillus' feelings on the day of
their departure? As a light-hearted tailpiece it can be interesting to ask
pupils which of their parents they might have had more chance of
'persuading' in such a situation.

Some pupils may ask about *ad lītus* (line 28) wondering why it is not *ad
lītum*; and this would be a useful moment to refer the class (*after* the story
has been finished) to the note on neuters in the Language Information
pamphlet, p.4.

astrologus victor

Now the tables are turned against Petro. Barbillus cannot in the end free
himself from the grip of superstition and the astrologer wins him over by
playing on his belief in the meaning of dreams. The death of Barbillus,
though reminiscent of the death of Caecilius, invites more mature

responses from pupils. The circumstances are more complex; there are no heroics, only the sadness of wisdom that comes too late. His final gesture makes reparation for the years of bitter refusal to forgive.

The picture on p.79 shows a papyrus letter from Prokleios to Pekysis, first century A.D. from Alexandria. The letter reads: 'Prokleios to his good friend Pekysis, greetings. You will do well if at your own risk you sell to my friend Sotas such high-quality goods as he will tell you he needs, for him to bring to me at Alexandria. Know that you will have to deal with me about the cost. Greet all your family from me. Farewell.'

Some suggested questions

Why should Barbillus, an apparently sensible and intelligent man, believe in astrology? Do you find such behaviour credible? (Reference might be made to the astrologer's good 'track record', judging by his successful predictions in 'vēnātiō', Stage 19, and in 'fortūna crūdēlis' in the present stage.)

What is it about astrology that you might regard as 'not sensible'? How might an astrologer ensure that his advice seemed reliable or at least plausible?

What is Quintus' attitude towards astrology? Do you think his attitude would have changed as a result of Barbillus' tragedy?

Why do you think Barbillus refused to let Quintus send for Petro?

What might the letter for Rufus have contained?

Second language note (oblique cases of is)

When the note has been read, consolidation should follow immediately. Ask pupils to pick out examples of the various forms of *is* from sentences already met, and make up further simple sentences for pupils to translate. Further consolidation activity could be based on the 'Pronouns' section of the Language Information pamphlet.

Manipulation exercises and suggestions for further practice

Exercise 1   Type: translation
             Linguistic feature being practised: relative clause
Encourage English equivalents for the Latin relative clause. Look out for signs of pupils' finding difficulty in determining the beginning or, more probably, the end of the clause. Although the punctuation offers help, some pupils are very prone to ignore clause boundaries, thereby distorting the meaning of the sentence. Careful reading aloud by the teacher, using pauses to emphasise the boundaries, is helpful. Note that the frequent use

of commas in the pupil's text to mark clause boundaries decreases in later stages.

Exercise 2   Type: comprehension
There are extant Latin wills, and in style this exercise is based on these. An attempt has also been made to make it look like an actual document, though in the interests of pupils' comprehension ancient script has not been reproduced and punctuation has been added. It is represented as a document on papyrus, like many wills found in Egypt; elsewhere, where papyrus was less plentiful, wax tablets were used. For the sealing of documents, remind pupils of Stage 4 'Hermogenēs' and 'in basilicā'.

The exercise includes further practice of the relative clause and of the dative. Pupils should be encouraged, in their answers to question 9, to be as particular as they can, e.g. 'fair rather than generous', 'truthful', 'realistic' etc. In addition to the questions in the pupil's text, the teacher might like to probe further by asking:

How do we know that Barbillus wholly trusted Quintus? (He assumed that Quintus would carry out a faithful search for Rufus, even though that was not in Quintus' own interests.)

How can we tell that the will was drawn up, at least in its final form, only a short time before Barbillus' death?

How many of the signatories were Roman citizens?

From one of the stories in this stage, pupils might be asked to pick out and identify examples of particular cases of nouns and/or adjectives, in the way described above on p.59, but now including examples of the genitive and dative cases. Then with the aid of the paradigm in the Language Information pamphlet, pp.4–5, able pupils could be invited to make up an English sentence which in Latin would have contained *servōrum* (or *cīvēs, urbī, puellīs* etc.) This exercise is less complicated than it sounds, and although lack of knowledge will inevitably produce some mistakes (e.g. the suggestion 'we went to the city' for *urbī*), it can be an effective reminder to pupils of the functions of the cases.

The background material

The main theme is that of medicine and pseudo-medicine. The short account given in the pupil's text may suffice for the present, but if further material is desired the teacher may refer to C.S.C.P. *The Romans discover Britain* 46–7 (translated source material) and the Teacher's Handbook, Singer, and Scarborough.

The Hippocratic oath is still discussed by doctors in the context of medical ethics, especially the sentence 'Whatever in my professional practice I see or hear, which ought not to be spoken abroad, I will not divulge.' With the growth of computerised records and ease of access to them, the issue of confidentiality has become more acute.

For other ethical problems, consider how far anatomical research can be combined with respect for the dead, or the modern controversies over heart transplants, test-tube babies, etc. On pseudo-medicine, a list of ancient remedies appears in Paoli 211–13 and C.S.C.P. *The Roman World* Unit II Item 82. If these remedies are met with derision or revulsion, invite pupils to reflect that even in the hands of the best doctors ancient surgery, apart from being expensive, must have been ugly and very painful (anaesthetics, where used at all, were extremely crude: the use of alcohol, narcotic drugs or knocking the patient unconscious). In view of this, might they have been more willing to try even the most unappetising 'folk cure' first? Superstition is discussed in the Teacher's Handbook to Unit IIIA.

For more information about Greek science generally the teacher might consult the following: Lee; Majno; Schools Council History Project; University of Bristol, *Illustrations* (which contains a number of very clear diagrams of calculations and inventions by Aristarchus, Eratosthenes, Archimedes, Ctesibius and Hero); Forster 32–46 (which offers some useful summaries of scholars' achievements); and Evans (which contains a number of excellent passages on medicine and science (pp.143–52) which might be read aloud to the class).

Suggestions for further work

1   Discuss some of the practical applications for the following devices that were used by Greeks and Romans: (a) pulley, (b) lever, (c) concave mirror, (d) cog wheels. When pupils have made their suggestions, refer to Archimedes and his devices for defending Syracuse. Some pupils may already be familiar with the two well-known anecdotes about his discovery of the principle of displacement and about his death.

2   Pupils might find out who were the most famous Alexandrian scholars and what they contributed to their particular fields.

3   Invite pupils to draw some of the Alexandrian inventions and explain how they worked.

The Language Information pamphlet

This pamphlet follows the same plan as its predecessors, and the general comments in Unit I Handbook p.81 continue to apply. The following notes are concerned with some specific points:

Nouns (pp.4–6). The vocative is now included in the table of nouns, and this may provoke comment or enquiry from pupils. Confirm their observations where appropriate; detailed discussion should be postponed until the relevant language note in Stage 19 is reached.

The gender of each noun is also indicated. *cīvis* has been classified here as masculine on grounds of frequency; if pupils ask whether it becomes feminine when referring to a female citizen, confirm that this is so.

The transformation exercise in paragraph 2 is fairly demanding (more so, in fact, than the exercise in paragraph 3; they are in that order so that paragraph 2 could be on the same page as the paradigm which pupils will need to refer to). Teachers will need to find, by experiment, the appropriate degree of help required by their pupils. For example, some teachers will wish to warn their class in advance about the word order of sentences 7 and 8; others will prefer to ask the class to comment after the sentences have been worked. (Specific practice in handling this word order is given later in the pamphlet, in paragraph 4 on page 19). For further notes on transformation exercises, see above, p.35

Adjectives (p.7). The examples in paragraph 4 might be discussed by the class; explanation of the reasons for a particular choice of inflection should normally come from the pupils rather than the teacher. Further examples on similar lines could be devised if necessary.

Pronouns (pp.11–13). The terms 'relative pronoun' and 'antecedent' are introduced in paragraph 7 of this sub-section: pupils might be asked to pick out examples of relative pronouns and antecedents from a story read previously, in addition to the examples in paragraph 7.

Verbs (pp.14–16). The present participle, described in Stage 20, is not included here, but will be discussed and practised at length, together with the perfect participle, in the Language Information pamphlet for Unit IIIA.

Irregular Verbs (pp.17–18). The perfect tense of *sum* is omitted from the table, as the pupils have not yet met it in their reading.

Word Order (pp.18–19). Further examples can be made up if additional practice is needed. The patterns in paragraphs 1 and 4 in particular may repay further practice in view of their relative frequency in original Latin literature. Of the examples in paragraph 6, pupils have met the pattern dative + accusative + verb from Stage 16 onwards, and dative + verb from Stage 17.

Longer Sentences I (pp.20–1). In these sentences, the subordinate clauses vary in four ways:

they are introduced by a variety of conjunctions;

their subject is sometimes the same as the subject of the main clause, and sometimes different;

they sometimes precede the main clause, sometimes follow it and sometimes interrupt it;

they include various additional complexities such as the prolate infinitive, the predicative use of the adjective, and the patterns dative + verb and dative + accusative + verb.

The exercise in paragraph 3 is fairly demanding. It may be helpful to have the clauses, and perhaps the sentences, translated orally in class before the pupils (working perhaps in groups) proceed with the matching-up. For sentence 5 in its completed form, encourage the translation 'As soon as the mother . . .' rather than 'The mother, as soon as she . . .'

Longer Sentences II (p.22). This sub-section begins with examples where a verb in the first of two parallel clauses has to be 'supplied' in the second; it continues with the harder (but more typically Latin) pattern in which a verb in the second clause must be 'supplied' in the first. Reading aloud by the teacher, with careful phrasing, will help pupils to grasp the point.

Words and phrases

It is worth spending a little time studying the introductory notes on pp.24–5 with the pupils and making sure that they can find their way round this section.

The exercise in paragraph 5 should be done orally; some pupils will need considerable help at first, and/or further practice afterwards. It may be advisable to end with some examples in complete sentences, in order to emphasise that the context usually lessens or even removes any difficulty. The difference in pronunciation between *flōris* and *fabrīs* should be noted.

Paragraph 6 might be followed by a little practice in looking up the nominative form of adjectives. Pupils could be asked to give the nominative singular, or the meaning, of (for example) *loquācēs; pulchrae; impigrī; īnsolentem.*

Linguistic synopsis of Unit IIB

For general comments, see Unit I Handbook p.84. LI = Language
Information pamphlet.

Stage	Linguistic feature	Place of language note etc.
17	genitive singular and plural (in prepositional phrases)	17, LI
	position of *tamen* (met from Stage 4), *igitur* (from	
	Stage 6) and *enim*	17
	obstō + dative	18
	DATIVE + VERB word order	LI
	ACCUSATIVE + NOMINATIVE + VERB word order	
	(one example)	LI
	increased incidence of VERB + NOMINATIVE word order	
	(from Stage 3)	LI
	increased complexity in subordinate clauses	LI
	pluperfect in main clause	
	clauses with *sīcut*	
	infinitive + *soleō, coepī, melius est*	
18	adjective (met from Stage 3): agreement of gender	18, LI
	cōnfīdō (from Stage 18), *obstō* (from Stage 17),	
	appropinquō, etc. + dative	18
	genitive + nominative	LI
	omission of verb in 1st of 2 clauses (met in Stage 15)	LI
	DATIVE + ACCUSATIVE + VERB word order (met in	
	Stage 16)	LI
	ACCUSATIVE + NOMINATIVE + VERB word order	
	(met in Stage 17)	LI
	ACCUSATIVE + VERB + NOMINATIVE word order	LI
	'branching' of one subordinate clause out of another	
	(e.g. *dīligenter labōrābant, quod aderat vīlicus,*	
	quī virgam vibrābat)	
	'nesting' of one subordinate clause inside another	
	(e.g. *ubi ā templō, in quō cēnāverat, domum redībat,*	
	amīcum cōnspexit accurrentem)	
	ACCUSATIVE + DATIVE + VERB word order	
	clauses with *ut* (= 'as')	

Stage	Linguistic feature	*Place of language note etc.*
19	*hic* (met from Stage 7)	19, LI
	imperative singular (from Stage 10) and plural (from Stage 14)	19, LI
	nōlī (from Stage 14) and *nōlīte*	19
	vocative (from Stages 11 and 14)	19, LI
	genitive + accusative	LI
	genitive of adjective	
	fīō + predicative nominative	
20	present participle (met from Stage 14)	20
	oblique cases of *is* (from Stage 7)	20, LI
	descriptive genitive (one example)	22
	'stringing' arrangement of 2 parallel subordinate clauses (e.g. *servī, quī Barbillum portābant, ubi cubiculum intrāvērunt, in lectum eum lēniter posuērunt*)	
	increased incidence of predicative adjective	

The following terms are used in Unit IIB. Numerals indicate the stage in which each term is introduced.

genitive	17
gender	18
masculine	18
feminine	18
neuter	18
imperative	19
vocative	19
present participle	20
relative pronoun	LI
antecedent	LI
1st, 2nd, 3rd person	LI

Appendix A: Attainment tests

For general comments, see Unit I Handbook, pp. 88–9. The words and phrases in heavy type are either new to the pupils or have occurred infrequently in the pupil's text up to the stage indicated.

Test 5

To be given at the end of Stage 18, preferably in two successive lessons.

ad pȳramidas

(a) Translate

ōlim Quīntus ad tabernam Clēmentis contendit. ubi ad tabernam pervēnit, Clēmentem salūtāvit.

'salvē, amīce', inquit. 'ego tibi aliquid dīcere volō. ad **pȳramidas** iter facere cupiō. sunt enim in Aegyptō multae pȳramides quās Aegyptiī ōlim **exstrūxērunt**. Aegyptiī in pȳramidibus rēgēs **sepelīre** solēbant. ego 5
pȳramidas vidēre volō quod sunt maximae et pulcherrimae. vīsne mēcum iter facere?'

Clēmēns laetus cōnsēnsit. itaque Quīntus et Clēmēns pecūniam et cibum in **saccīs** posuērunt. tum ad Plūtum, mercātōrem Graecum, festīnāvērunt et **camēlōs condūxērunt.** saccōs, quōs ē tabernā Clēmentis 10
portāverant, in camēlīs posuērunt. tum camēlōs **cōnscendērunt** et ex urbe discessērunt. per agrōs et vīllās prōcēdēbant.

subitō decem Aegyptiī, quī **insidiās** parāverant, impetum fēcērunt. Quīntus et Clēmēns fortiter resistēbant sed facile erat Aegyptiīs eōs superāre quod fūstēs ingentēs habēbant. tum Aegyptiī cum pecūniā et 15
camēlīs effūgērunt. Quīntus et Clēmēns trīstēs ad urbem reveniēbant.

'ēheu!' inquit Clēmēns. 'quam miserī sumus! pȳramidas nōn vīdimus: pecūniam et camēlōs āmīsimus.'

(b) Read the rest of the story and, without translating, answer the questions at the end.

Quīntus et Clēmēns per urbem fessī prōcēdēbant. ubi tabernam Plūtī praeterībant, rem mīrābilem vīdērunt. camēlī, quōs Aegyptiī 20
abdūxerant, extrā tabernam Plūtī stābant! tum Quīntus rem tōtam intellēxit. amīcī īrātī mercātōrem quaesīvērunt, sed invenīre nōn poterant. aderat tamen puer parvus quī camēlōs custōdiēbat. Quīntus puerō clāmāvit,

'heus, tū! ubi sunt Aegyptiī quī in nōs impetum fēcērunt? ego eōs dē 25 pecūniā meā **interrogāre** volō.'

puer perterritus 'rogā Plūtum', inquit, et statim fūgit.

amīcī per viās Alexandrīae Plūtum frūstrā quaesīvērunt. tandem thermās intrāvērunt. ecce! Plūtus in palaestrā cum **duōbus** servīs ambulābant. Quīntus servōs agnōvit. eōs enim vīderat in turbā Aegyptiōrumn quī impetum fēcerant. Quīntus ad Plūtum prōcessit, quī, postquam eum īrātum vīdit, valdē timēbat. Quīntus clāmāvit,

'ubi est mea pecūnia? camēlōs iam invēnimus!'

Plūtus erat perterritus quod Quīntus erat cīvis Rōmānus. Plūtus Quīntō '**ignōsce** mihi', inquit. 'ego tibi pecūniam libenter reddō et parvum dōnum tibi offerō.'

deinde Quīntum et Clēmentem ad vīllam suam dūxit. ibi eīs duōs equōs dedit. Quīntus numquam equōs pulchriōrēs quam illōs vīderat! tum Quīntus et Clēmēns equōs cōnscendērunt et ad pȳramidas laetī contendērunt.

1 How were Quintus and Clemens feeling when they got back to the city?
2 How did they know they were on the track of the thieves?
3 What question did Quintus ask the boy?
4 What did the boy reply?
5 Where was Plutus and what was he doing when Quintus and Clemens found him?
6 What did Quintus notice about the slaves attending Plutus?
7 Why was Plutus so frightened when Quintus told him about the camels?
8 What happened when Plutus took Quintus and Clemens to his house?
9 What did Quintus think of Plutus' present?
10 How does the story end?

Test 6

To be given at the end of Stage 20, preferably in two successive lessons.

testāmentum Barbillī

(a) Translate

multī amīcī cum Galatēā et Aristōne cēnābant. dē morte Barbillī colloquium habēbant.

'magnum **lēgātum** exspectō', inquit Galatēa. 'nam ubi Barbillus aeger iacēbat, eum cotīdiē vīsitābam. magnam partem diēī cum eō **cōnsūmēbam**.'

omnēs Galatēam laudāvērunt et clāmāvērunt,

'decōrum est tibi praemium **meritum** accipere.'

Petrō, medicus Graecus, triclīnium intrāvit. Galatēa, ubi eum
cōnspexit, īrāta surrēxit et rogāvit,
  'cūr hūc vēnistī? nōs omnēs tē **dēspicimus**, quod tū Barbillum sānāre   10
nōn poterās.'
  'ego hūc vēnī, quod tibi aliquid dīcere volō', respondit Petrō.
  'quid est?' rogāvit Galatēa.
  '**testāmentum** Barbillī vīdī', respondit ille.
  Galatēa, ubi hoc audīvit, **īram dēposuit.** Petrōnem in mediōs amīcōs   15
dūxit et cibum vīnumque eī obtulit.
  'ō **dulcissime**', inquit Galatēa, 'quam libenter tē vidēmus. **dīc** nōbīs
quam celerrimē dē testāmentō! quid Barbillus nōbīs relīquit?'

(b) Read the rest of the story and, without translating, answer the
questions at the end.

  omnēs tacuērunt et Petrōnem intentē audīvērunt.
  'Barbillus Aristōnī nūllam pecūniam relīquit', inquit Petrō, 'sed   20
tragoediās, quās Aristō scrīpsit, reddidit.'
  amīcī statim rīsērunt quod tragoediae Aristōnis pessimae erant.
Galatēa quoque rīsit.
  'optimē fēcit Barbillus', inquit Galatēa. 'Barbillus Aristōnī tragoediās
sōlum relīquit quod Aristō nihil aliud cūrat. **sine dubiō** Barbillus mihi   25
multam pecūniam relīquit quod ego **prūdentior** sum quam marītus
meus.'
  tum Petrō Galatēae dīxit, 'Barbillus fīliae tuae gemmās, quās ā
mercātōre Arabī ēmit, relīquit.'
  'quam fortūnāta est Helena!' exclāmāvērunt amīcī.   30
  Galatēa hanc rem graviter ferēbat.
  'nōn decōrum est Helenae gemmās habēre. nam Helena est stultior
quam pater. **tūtius est** Helenae gemmās mihi trādere. sed cūr nihil dē mē
dīcis, Petrō? quid Barbillus mihi relīquit?'
  Petrō tamen nihil respondit.   35
  'dīc mihi, stultissime', inquit Galatēa īrāta.
  tandem Petrō susurrāvit, 'nihil tibi relīquit.'
  omnēs amīcī valdē commōtī erant: multī cachinnāvērunt, paucī
lacrimāvērunt.
  Galatēa tamen tacēbat. **humī** dēciderat exanimāta.   40

1 What did Aristo receive in the will?
2 What did Galatea's friends do when they heard what Aristo had
     received?
3 What, according to Galatea, was Aristo's only interest in life?
4 What did Galatea hope to receive herself?
5 Why did Galatea's friends describe Helena as 'fortūnāta'?
6 Why is the Arab merchant mentioned?

7 What does Galatea think about her daughter's character?
8 What does she think her daughter should do?
9 From Petro's behaviour at the end of the story, find two reasons for supposing that he was embarrassed about telling Galatea what she had received.
10 What did Galatea receive?
11 How did most of Galatea's friends show their feelings about this? How did a few of them behave?
12 What effect did the news have on Galatea?

Part (a) of this test can be used to assess, amongst other things, pupils' ability to handle the 1st and 2nd person inflections of the verb in various tenses. The teacher may also wish to note how they cope with the omission of the subject in *Petrōnem . . . dūxit et cibum . . . obtulit* (lines 15–16). If pupils produce 'the will which Barbillus has left us' for line 18, discussion of the punctuation of the Latin may give them a clearer understanding of where they went wrong than analysis of the difference between 'quid' and 'quod'.

Vocabulary tested in part (b) includes *rīdēre* (cf. question 2), *nihil aliud* (question 3), *emere* (question 6) and *cachinnāre* (question 11). In answering question 9, pupils have not only to understand the text but also to draw inferences from it; such exploration of the text could be taken further in oral discussion after the test has been completed. For example, the class might be asked to pick out, and suggest explanations for, Galatea's change of tone from '*ō dulcissime*' in line 17 of part (a) to '*dīc mihi, stultissime*' in line 36 of part (b).

Appendix B: Words and phrases in Unit IIB checklists

The numeral indicates the stage in which the word or phrase appears in a checklist.

ā (='from') (17)
adīre (20)
aliquid (18)
amāre (19)
animus (17)
appropinquāre (17)
āra (17)
arcessere (20)
ars (20)
audēre (18)
auris (20)

bene (17)
benignus (17)

caedere (19)
caput (18)
cārus (19)
castīgāre (19)
cautē (19)
coepisse (13)
cōgitāre (19)
cognōscere (18)
collocāre (20)
comparāre (19)
cōnficere (19)
cōnsistere (18)
crūdēlis (20)
cūrāre (19)

dē (='down from')(19)
dea (18)
decem (20)
dēfendere (19)
dēmōnstrāre (18)
dēnique (20)

dēsilīre (17)
dēspērāre (17)
discēdere (18)
diū (17)
doctus (20)
domus (20)
dulcis (19)
duo (12 & 20)

equitāre (20)
exanimātus (17)

facilis (17)
fīlia (19)
fluere (19)
fortasse (18)
forte (19)
fortūna (18)
frangere (18)
fulgēre (17)

gemma (17)
grātiās agere (19)
graviter (17)

haerēre (17)
hasta (17)
hiems (20)
hūc (17)

ibi (18)
illūc (19)
impetus (17)
īnferre (20)
īnsula (17)
invītus (18)
irrumpere (20)

itaque (17)
iter (19)

latrō (17)
lātus (20)
libenter (18)
līberāre (20)
locus (19)
longus (18)
lūna (20)

māne (19)
manus (='hand')(18)
mare (17)
maximus (17)
medicus (20)
mīles (18)
mors (20)
multitūdō (17)

nam (18)
neglegēns (19)
negōtium (17)
nēmō (18)
novem (20)
nōvisse (19)
nox (18)
numquam (17)

obstāre (18)
octō (20)
oculus (20)

parēns (20)
pars (18)
paucī (17)
perīculōsus (18)

Words and phrases

perīculum (19)
persuādēre (20)
pervenīre (17)
pessimus (20)
petere (='beg for')(18)
plūrimī (19)
plūrimus (19)
pompa (19)
poscere (19)
posteā (18)
postrēmō (18)
praesidium (18)
precēs (20)
prō (18)
prōcumbere (18)

recipere (17)
recūsāre (18)
relinquere (20)
remedium (20)
resistere (18)

sacer (18)
saevīre (18)
septem (20)
sermō (20)
sex (20)
sīcut (20)
sine (17)
solēre (17)
sonitus (19)
sordidus (17)
stola (19)

umerus (19)
ūnus (12 & 20)

vexāre (19)
vīgintī (20)
vīta (17)
vīvere (19)
vix (19)
vōx (19)
vulnus (20)

quadrāgintā (20)
quattuor (20)
quīnquāgintā (20)
quīnque (20)
quō? (18)
quondam (17)

tam (20)
temptāre (20)
tergum (17)
tot (19)
trēs (12 & 20)
trīgintā (20)

Appendix C: Summary of changes from the first edition of the course

Changes in Unit IIB include the following:

1 New **vocabulary** has been reduced by about 25 words and the total length of the **reading material** by about 60 lines.

2 A little more variation of word order has been introduced into the **linguistic scheme**. For example, the sentence pattern accusative + nominative + verb is now included, and also occasional examples, such as *Clēmēns vir fortis, nōn senex īnfirmus est*, where the verb has to be 'supplied' in the first, rather than the second, of two clauses. The number of present participles has been increased.

3 New **model sentences** have been written for Stages 18,19 and 20.

4 New **language notes** include notes dealing with gender, various pronouns, the present participle, the imperative and the vocative.

5 The **background material** for Stages 17,18 and 19 has been extensively rewritten.

6 The genitive of the noun has been included in the '**Words and phrases checklists**' and the 'Words and phrases' section of the **Language Information pamphlet.**

7 An additional **attainment test** is included to follow Stage 18.

Bibliography

Books

Books marked * are suitable for pupils. Some of the others would also be suitable for pupils to refer to under the teacher's guidance. Some recommended out-of-print (O.P.) books are included in case teachers already possess them or can obtain second-hand copies.

General

Cambridge Ancient History, vol.XI (C.U.P. 1936)
Cambridge School Classics Project. *The Roman World* Units I and II (C.U.P. 1978–9)
Lewis, N. and Reinhold, M. *Roman Civilisation: a Sourcebook, II The Empire* (Harper Torchbooks: Harper and Row 1966)
McEvedy, C. *Penguin Atlas of Ancient History* (Penguin 1970)
Paoli, U.E. *Rome, its People, Life and Customs* (Longman 1963)

Alexandria and trade

Badian, E. *'Ancient Alexandria' History Today* 10, November 1960
Evans, I.O. *Gadget City: A Story of Ancient Alexandria* (Warne 1944 O.P.)
    A novel about a Welsh slave, captured in Britain and sent to work at the Museum in Alexandria.
Forster, E.M. *Alexandria: a history and guide* 2nd edn by M.von Haag (M. Haag 1981)
Fraser, P.M. *Ptolemaic Alexandria,* 3 vols. (O.U.P. 1972)
Hodge, P. *Roman Trade and Travel* (Longman 1978)
Lindsay, J. *Daily Life in Roman Egypt* (Muller 1963 O.P.)
    Leisure and Pleasure in Roman Egypt (Muller 1965 O.P.)
Marlowe, J. *The Golden Age of Alexandria* (Gollancz 1971 O.P.)
Meiggs, R. *Roman Ostia* (O.U.P. 2nd edn 1974 O.P.)
Thorley, J. 'The Silk Trade between China and the Roman Empire at its Height, circa A.D. 90–130' *Greece and Rome* n.s.18, April 1971

Religion

Apuleius. *The Golden Ass* tr. R. Graves (Penguin 1972)
Ferguson, J. *The Religions of the Roman Empire* (Aspects of Greek and Roman Life series: Thames & Hudson 1970 O.P.)

Gwyn Griffiths, J. *The Isis-Book* (Apuleius, *Metamorphoses* XI) (Brill 1975)
Lindsay, J. *Men and Gods on the Roman Nile* (Muller 1968 O.P.)
  Origins of Astrology (Muller 1970 O.P.)
Robertson, O. *Rite of Rebirth: Initiation of the Fellowship of Isis*
  (Cesara Publications, Huntington Castle, Clonegal, Enniscorthy,
  Eire, 1977)
Witt, R.E. *Isis in the Graeco-Roman World* (Aspects of Greek and Roman
  Life series: Thames & Hudson 1971 O.P.)

Medicine, science and technology

Clagett, M. *Greek Science in Antiquity* (Arno 1977)
Cambridge School Classics Project. *The Romans Discover Britain* (C.U.P.
  1981)
Davies, R.W. 'Medicine in Ancient Rome' *History Today* 21, November
  1971
Dodsworth, R. *Glass and Glassmaking* (Shire Publications 1982) A short
  illustrated history.
Farrington, B. *Greek Science: its meaning for us* (Spokesman Books 1981)
Green, M. *Roman Technology and Crafts* (Aspects of Roman Life series:
  Longman 1979)
Harden, D.B. *Ancient Glass II: Roman*. Reprint from *The Archaeological
  Journal* CXXVI (available from the Royal Archaeological Institute,
  c/o 304 Addison House, Grove End Road, London NW8 9EL)
Hodges, H. *Technology in the Ancient World* (Allen Lane 1970 O.P.)
Hull, L.W.H. *History and Philosophy of Science* (Longman 1959 O.P.)
Landels, J. *Engineering in the Ancient World* (Chatto & Windus 1978)
Lee, Sir D. 'Science, Philosophy and Technology in the Greco-Roman
  World' *Greece and Rome* n.s. 20, April, October 1973
Majno, G. *The Healing Hand: Man and Wound in the Ancient World* (Harvard
  University Press 1975)
Scarborough, J. *Roman Medicine* (Aspects of Greek and Roman Life series:
  Thames & Hudson 1969 O.P.)
Schools Council 13–16 History Project *Medicine through Time, Vol.I: Early
  Man and Medicine* – and its associated filmstrip (Holmes McDougall
  1976)
Singer, C. *Greek Biology and Greek Medicine* (O.U.P. 1922 O.P.)
Strong, D. and Brown, D. (eds.) *Roman Crafts* (Duckworth 1976)
University of Bristol, School of Education. *Illustrations of Astronomy,
  Science and Technology in the Alexandrian Age* (Obtainable from JACT
  Hon. Publications Secretary, Dr. J. Roy, 20 Hallam Grange Croft,
  Sheffield, S10 4BP)

Bibliography
Filmstrips

No filmstrip is devoted wholly to Roman Alexandria, but the following
may provide background material.
  Addresses of suppliers are given at the end of this list.

Bolton, P.H. *Ancient Egypt: The Gift of the Nile* and *Empire and Decay*. Two
filmstrips, double-frame, colour, 44 and 41 frames, full notes and teaching
suggestions, optional cassette. Photographs of the Egyptian landscape, art
and monuments, with some diagrams and reconstructions, outline the
history, life and art of Egypt up to Cleopatra VII. Only the last three
frames deal with the period from Alexander the Great, and none with the
Roman occupation, but the photography is often exciting and there are
useful frames showing, for example, the Nile, Isis and Osiris, boats.
(Visual Publications M4/1,M4/2)

Neurath, M. *Life in Ancient Egypt*. Filmstrip, single-frame, colour,
27 frames + titles, notes. Attractive colour diagrams based on Egyptian
paintings. Sequence on flooding of the Nile. Not the Roman period.
(Longman/Common Ground 07056 06805)

Parks, A. and M. *People of Other Days: Life in Ancient Egypt I and II*. Two
filmstrips, single-frame, colour, 34 and 36 frames, full notes. From a series
chiefly intended for younger pupils, these strips are composed of bold and
clear artist's reconstructions, with maps. The first gives a bird's-eye view
of Egypt's history from 2600 B.C. to the Romans. One frame shows the
Alexandrian Pharos. The second strip includes daily life of ordinary
Egyptians, farming and building, papyrus, and hunting on the Nile
marshes, as well as subjects less relevant to the Cambridge Latin Course.
(Visual Publications PD 18, 19).

Sudhalter, R, *et al. Religion in Roman Life*. Filmstrip, single-frame, colour,
89 frames, notes, cassette or tape. Teachers may prefer to use this strip as
a whole, with its own sound, as it is imaginatively planned to give an
effect rather like a film. One could select the section on Isis and Mithras.
Visuals are taken from Roman reliefs, paintings, mosaics etc., with some
photographs of lightning and other phenomena. (E.A.V.)

Addresses of suppliers

Educational Audio Visual Ltd., Mary Glasgow Publications Ltd.,
   Brookhampton Lane, Kineton, Warwick, CV35 0JB
Longman Group Ltd., Longman House, Burnt Mill, Harlow, Essex
   CM20 2JE
Visual Publications, The Green, Northleach, Cheltenham GL54 3EX